The Complete
Bouvier des Flandres

Chet Collier's AKC Ch. Naris du Posty Arlequin, the record holding show winner in the United States. Photo by Gilbert.

The Complete Bouvier des Flandres

by Claire D. McLean

with contributions by
    Edmee Bowles
    Justin Chastel
    Chet Collier
    Murray Horowitz, M.D.
    Marion Hubbard
    Carl B. May, Jr.
    Lil Mees
    Club du Bouvier des Flandres pour la France
    Club National Belge du Bouvier des Flandres

edited by Herm David

1974

Dreenan Press Ltd.

Croton-on-Hudson, New York 10520

© 1974 by Claire D. McLean
All rights reserved.
Printed in the United States of America.
No part of this publication may be reproduced,
stored in a retrieval system, or transmitted, in any form
or by any means, electronic, mechanical, photocopying, recording or
otherwise, without the prior written permission of the publisher.

Library of Congress Catalog Card Number:74-75115

ISBN: 0-88376-050-9

This book was typeset by University Graphics,
and printed and bound by The Maple Press.

CONTENTS

	In Appreciation	vii
	Preface	ix
1.	The Bouvier des Flandres and His Predecessors	11
2.	The Bouvier Comes to America	55
3.	The Role of the Bouvier Clubs	71
4.	The Belgian Challenge and the Dorothy Walsh Trophies	75
5.	European Kennels	79
6.	Importing a Bouvier	93
7.	Belco and I, by Aimee Bowles	103
8.	Some American Kennels	115
9.	The Breed's Standards	145
10.	Breeding Bouviers, Whelping and Raising the Litter, by Mary Hubbard	169
11.	Grooming Your Bouvier, by Lil Mees	181
12.	The Bouvier in Obedience	191
13.	The Bouvier in Art, by Murray Horowitz, M.D.	197
14.	Campaigning a Bouvier, by Chet Collier	203
15.	On the Character of the Bouvier des Flandres, by Justin Chastel	207

16. Bouviers in the Service of Man	209
17. Bouvier Records and Statistics, compiled by Carl B. May, Jr.	223
Appendix of Pedigrees	245

Photo by Stephanie Rancou

In Appreciation

Miss Edmee Bowles, an activist in the Belgian underground, was forced to flee her native land. She had trained fifteen Bouviers to guard against and to attack Nazis. She, her mother and their Bouvier, Belco, managed to escape to the United States. Here she continued her struggle against the Nazis by assisting the Dogs for Defense program as an advisor, as a trainer and as a breeder. She has never stopped serving others. No Bouvier breeder in North America can recall a time when Miss Bowles wasn't helping others to know, breed, show, train, love and enjoy Bouviers. Her companion in this photo is Bel Echo du Clos des Cerberes.

The author, left, her sister, Ginger, and Max, their first Bouvier, in 1943. Bred by Mrs. Louis deRochemont, Max had small, uncropped ears. Photo by Ray Marshall.

PREFACE

I was just a small girl when my aunt, Mrs. Dorothy Walsh, inducted me into the cult of the Bouvier by presenting me with Max. He was more than just a dog. He was my pal, and in many ways a gentle and persuasive teacher. He felt his mission in life was to guard me from all those dangers a child doesn't recognize. Whenever I went wandering off, which I did so often, Max was always there at my heels.

In a very real sense this book is Dorothy Walsh's final contribution to Bouviers. She gathered much of the material over a period of years. She believed there was a need for a book about the Bouvier and she encouraged me in my efforts. I had hoped to present her with the first bound copy, but that was not to be. However I can and do dedicate *The Complete Bouvier des Flandres* to her memory.

It seems the entire Bouvier community—worldwide—has joined in the preparation of this first true book on the Bouvier. I couldn't possibly list here all who are deserving of thanks. Whenever feasible contributions of information and illustrations are acknowledged in the text.

Every effort has been made to be both inclusive and accurate. These are objectives which, while approachable, are never fully attainable. Suggestions, additions and corrections are solicited and will be gratefully received.

If this book introduces new people to the joys and the practical advantages of a Bouvier's companionship—if it brings added enjoyment to those who already own Bouviers—then it will have been worthwhile.

Claire McLean

Chester Springs, Pennsylvania
April, 1974

THE BOUVIER DES FLANDRES AND HIS PREDECESSORS

MOST dog histories are necessarily conjecture and surmise. That is because the dog's alliance with man began long before man began to write and record the events of his emergence from the jungle. We know the alliance is at least 9,300 years old because the most careful carbon dating of surrounding artifacts in a human habitation digging in Star Carr, England places dog bones found there at 7,300 years B.C. Researchers reported man may have already domesticated some other animals.

We cannot know whether the dog was man's first conquest from the animal world, nor can we know which was the dog's first service to man. It may have been as a partner in the hunt—an enterprise in which the capabilities of canine and human still compliment each other. It may have been as a guard. A group of wild dogs bedded down near a cave in hopes of sharing in man's "table scraps" might signal by bark, howl or otherwise the approach of an intruder. The dog's service as a scavenger was necessary. The cave man who made a kill had no refrigeration. Meat he couldn't eat attracted disease-bearing insects and bacteria—and dangerous predators. In parts of India and the Middle East packs of semi-wild dogs continue to serve as the sewerage and sanitary disposal systems. The daily experience of seeing dogs eating human offal may explain the historic—and even religious—rejection of the dog by most peoples of this part of the world.

Somewhere early in their alliance against the deadly perils of their world man and dog discovered they had become more to each other than partners in struggles for survival. They discovered they enjoyed each other's companionship. The probability is that dogs were serving primitive man as hunting partners, guards, scavengers and companions. Then, we can rather safely assume, man invented a little-heralded device which made the domestication and utilization of animals possible and made an agrarian economy possible for him. He learned how to tie a knot!

The knot made it possible for man to hold an animal and to guide it into doing his bidding. Those that refused were probably beaten to death in the "guiding" process. A first factor in human selection of breeding stock was thus introduced. With his knot man could, for the first time, become a "breeder." He could select mates for the animals he held—and he surely chose those animals which most exhibited the qualities which he saw as being most useful to himself. If we are searching for the beginings of any of today's breeds of dogs we can start with the first time a man led his bitch over to the next valley so she could be covered by a stud he admired that belonged to a neighbor.

Other livestock was, by human criteria, "improved" in the same manner. But, a man can hold only a limited number of animals on a string. If he ties them out they are completely defenseless and easy prey for all kinds of marauders. Prehistoric man couldn't expand his holdings until he had developed a dog he could confidently unleash and depend upon to guard other varieties of livestock.

We will never know where or when man first confidently entrusted his livestock to the vigilance of a dog—but that is where we must date the beginings of the Bouvier and every other stock dog.

In time—and it must have taken hundreds of dog generations—man had, in various parts of his world, breeds of specialist dogs that could not only be depended upon to guard his livestock but to help him control and contain it so that it no longer had to be tied out or penned. The process of improving stock dogs by selective breeding continues today.

Geographic isolation forced men to select breeding stock from animals easily available to them. Thus, because the introduction of "outside" blood was nearly impossible, regional "types" or "breeds", recognizable because of a certain uniformity of appearance emerged. It is interesting to note that breeds of stock dogs with the same jobs to do, i.e., over similar terrain and in similar weather conditions, although evolved independently of each other, display considerable similarity in size, weight, temperament and talents.

As man became more specialized so did his dogs. Stock dogs were sorted out into herding and droving dogs. And, there have always been some that did both jobs rather well for farmers with both sheep and cattle but only enough prosperity to support one dog.

The beginnings of the Bouvier are hardly better documented than are the beginnings of domestic dogs or stock dogs or drovers' dogs. They don't need to be. The Bouvier des Flandres of today is a proud, practical dog of distinctive, commanding appearance. He is an honest dog that needs no breed history reaching into antiquity. It would be inappropriate and beneath the Bouvier's dignity to here paste fabricated spangles onto his past.

Through all of their history the Flemings of his native land have proven themselves among the most skilled, practical animal breeders of the world. Through hundreds of years and many thousands of dog generations they utilized that skill in developing the Bouvier and his predecessors.

The development of the Bouvier into the handsome, useful and engaging companion that he is today has had its heroes and its perilous episodes. World War I, which so bloodied the meadows of Flanders, almost meant extinction for the Bouvier. At great personal sacrifice his dedicated supporters somehow managed to bring the best of the breeding stock through. Exploding shells and occupying armies, hunger and death, thoroughly tested their devotion to their native breed. Because only the best could be kept there was an *imposed* stringent selection and the net result was vastly accelerated "purification" and development of the modern Bouvier.

If we are to understand the origins of the Bouvier, if we wish to begin at the beginning, we must first know something of the people and the land where he evolved.

Courtesy Belgian National Tourist Office.

The Matin has either been a type rather than a breed—or a breed without type. This 1750 engraving by Moitte from a drawing by DeSeve is from *Buffon's Natural History* published in Paris. From the editor's collection.

The low countries, Holland and Belgium, are small. Together they are less than half the size of New York state—with about 11% more population (22.2 million). They comprise one of the most densely populated places on earth. The area is intensively farmed but as in most industrial-commercial societies the percentage of the work force in agriculture has been declining steadily since about 1930. Today in Belgium, for example, only about one in twenty of the work force is farming, even though farms occupy about 53% of the land area. This decline in the number of farm families has resulted in a proportionate decrease in the number of farm dogs. Some native types which survived the two world wars have either failed or are failing to survive modern agricultural technology. Only those breeds, such as the Bouvier, which have been adopted and popularized by show-minded enthusiasts have prospered.

Belgium is a country where two of Europe's ancient cultures, Germanic and Gaelic, meet. It has four languages and as many subcultures. The official government figures show 3,130,000 Walloons living in the southern provinces bordering France and speaking their variation of the French language, about 1,080,000 urbane Belgians living in the Brussels area and speaking a purer French, 61,000

This is the Matin as it was depicted in Eugene Gayot's 1867 Paris book, *Le Chen, Historie Naturelle*. From the editor's collection.

This more modern Matin was portrayed in *Toepoel's Honden Encyclopaedie*, published in Amsterdam, circa 1950. From the editor's collection.

The "Matin Belge" has been found in a variety of coats. He has also been known as "le chien de truit." From the collection of Miss Edmee Bowles.

Also from Gayot's *Le Chien* of 1867, another variation of the Matin, Obviously the breed served bakers as well as dairymen. From the editor's collection.

German-speaking people living along the German border, and 5,374,000 residents of the Flemish provinces of West Vlaanderen and Oost (East) Vlaanderen where the language is a minor variation of Dutch.

The Flemings comprise about 55% of the Belgian population but, because the international boundary was drawn on religious rather than ethnic lines, they also populate the Dutch province of Zeeland. Brugge is the capital of West Vlaanderen, Ghent of Oost Vlaanderen and Middleburg of Zeeland. Ghent is easily the largest of the three.

Flanders' buffer-area status and its strategic military and economic value have made a battleground of the territory since prehistoric times. Through the centuries the Flemings have, as fiercely as necessary, persisted in preserving their language, customs, liberty and identity. They have survived Caesar and the Romans, invasions by Teutonic tribes and Islamic forces, governments of the Franks, Charlemagne and the Holy Roman Empire, and further invasions by Norsemen. They have endured rule of varying oppressiveness by the Burgundians, the French, Austrian and Spanish princes.

The sum of these brought Belgium to what it calls "The Century of Misfortune," 1621–1715. For those 95 years the country was a battlefield between the Hapsburgs and the Bourbons. Between 1715 and

1792 Austrian Emperors ruled through governors. There followed two years of independence before the French revolutionaries annexed Belgium in 1794. That occupation ended with Napoleon's disaster in Russia. But then he came back to spill more blood at Waterloo, about eight miles south of Brussels.

For the next 15 years Belgium was a part of the United Kingdom of the Netherlands. But there were religious and other differences and the Kingdom of Belgium was proclaimed on October 4, 1830. There followed nearly a century of neutrality, but this was violated by the German armies in 1914. Belgium again became the world's bloodiest battleground. In 1940 Hitler invaded. Again Belgium fought a delaying action and lost many men before accepting occupation. The German regime brought extreme privation and terror.

The Belgian underground undermined the Nazi rulers until the Allied armies arrived in 1944. Once again Belgium became a bloody battleground as the stubborn Nazis were fought back beyond their own borders.

The Flemings are proud and enduring, hard working and peaceful, but fierce when aroused. They are responsible and resourceful with an extremely strong sense of territory. And, that is also a rather accurate description of the dog they developed—the Bouvier des Flandres!

It is not surprising that a people and their dogs should be so similar in basic characteristics. The land makes the same demands of both.

The Flemings did not create the Bouvier by design. They had needs which they tried to fill, one breeding at a time, one puppy selection at a time, over a period of centuries.

Belgians are a practical people with practical dogs. In this rare World War I photo a four-dog team draws a gun carriage as part a "cart" which seems improvised from bicycle parts. The chest over the front axle probably carried the shells. From the collection of the late Janet W. Mack.

When war comes to Belgians all of their resources are utilized to repel the invaders. Here is a dog-drawn World War I ambulance cart. Note the dog's cobby body and his blocky head. he seems an intermediary between the Matin and the Bouvier. From the collection of the late Janet W. Mack.

Farmers are not ordinarily sentimental about animals. How can they be when they raise so many to be butchered as cash crops? In a sense farm dogs are both hired hands and animals. As hired hands they must earn their keep. As animals they are expendable if they do not. Selection is practical, harsh, *and effective*.

Farmers cannot afford to support overly specialized breeds of dogs. On almost any family farm, anywhere, a dog must be whatever he is needed to be. In Flanders he has had to be effective as a guard dog, watch dog, herder, drover, cart puller, butter churner, vermin eliminator—and family companion. With all of that he has had to be hardy enough to live outdoors in all kinds of weather. Again, that is a pretty good description of the Bouvier!

If we are to deal properly with the history of the Bouvier as a "breed" we must first explore a concept little known to the world of dog shows. Until quite recent times virtually all Bouvier breeders selected only for performance qualities, not appearance factors. They were interested in what a dog could do and what was in his head and heart—and not very much in what he looked like. Thus while the Bouvier has a long and honorable history, he entered this century without that uniformity of appearance which dog show folks refer to as "type." His genetics were pure for what he could do and mixed for size and color, length and texture of coat.

This concept might be easier to understand if an analogous situation is cited. Over the world there are several Border Collie registries. All but one of them require a working certificate for both sire and dam before a puppy can be registered. The breed standard is performance and there is no written appearance standard. (The exception is a tangential group of admirers seeking American Kennel Club recognition for the breed.) Most Border Collie breeders believe a conformation standard could only serve to deemphasize working qualities.

However, when priorities *must* be assigned, survival must supercede an effort to achieve perfection. As we have seen, the Bouvier would probably be as extinct today as are some of the other "breed types" of the area if dedicated "show" breeders had not at great personal sacrifice brought a few of the best specimens through two devastating wars.

Instead of being hitched in pairs these cart dogs are harnessed four abreast to haul this Belgian merchant's cart. Note the lantern for night driving. It must have been a hot day for these Matin-type dogs. The proprietor's clothing places the photo in the World War I era. From the collection of the late Janet W. Mack.

After their first appearances at dog shows very early in this century Bouviers became a minor sensation. Admirers began combing Flemish farmlands all of the way to the North Sea in searches for breeding stock. What they found was variety insofar as appearance was concerned. Using the word in another sense, they found several "types" of Chien de Bouvier, literally, in French, "dog of the herdsman."

As dog shows gained popularity early in this century prideful Belgians were anxious to discover admirable native breeds—and they did. But this effort involved them in the differences between "breed" and "type". Because they didn't understand the differences (Genetics was only in its beginnings as a science) they were understandably inclined to label "types" as "breeds." Littermates of dissimilar appearance could acquire equally dissimilar "breed" designations. International borders and national prides further complicated the nomenclature procedure. One result was that a regional, functional "type" was sorted out into several breeds.

The world's greatest dog registries still do not agree upon a definition of the term "breed." Most of them were "locked in" on their definitions and concepts before genetics became a viable field of study. If the early show enthusiasts introduced some confusion by designating "types" as "breeds" it is forgivable. But if we wish to understand the Bouvier's history we should have our own look at the situation.

It would probably be close to the truth to surmise that the first breeders of the modern Bouvier selected from a regional, functional "type," individuals of similar appearance and size; then through careful breeding, fixed those appearance and temperament factors most important to them. The result has been an animal which is now a "breed" by *anyone's* definition. That animal is the Bouvier we know and treasure today.

Some of the other "types" failed to survive the two world wars because they lacked supporters willing to make the considerable sacrifices necessary to carry breeding stock through periods of battleground devastation interspersed with longer intervals of hunger and privation under enemy occupation. Because the Bouvier had won the loyalties of a band of dedicated breeders the Bouvier survived—and eventually prospered.

The Bouvier fared better in Holland during the first World War because of that country's neutrality. Hitler's Nazis of World War

In the photo at top another Matin-type dog is hitched to a rather heavily-laden milk cart with big, iron-banded wooden wheels. At bottom another of the Matin-type is hitched to the Count de T'Serclaes' riding cart. From the collection of the late Janet W. Mack.

II devastated all of the Bouvier's homeland—Holland, Belgium and northern France.

That is our own, historian's, overview. It is not necessary—and probably not even desirable—that historians agree.

Specific history must be pieced together from surviving documents and photos and from incomplete published articles. Again, the wars destroyed much documentation.

Helpful is a pre-World War article in the Flemish magazine *Culture* by L. Huyghbaert. So are later articles in another Belgian magazine, *L'Aboi*. Some of those who wrote on the Bouvier for *L'Aboi* were Messrs Charles Huge, A. Gevaert and Dr. Domicent. Before World War II Messrs Wolfs and Meyer wrote of the Bouvier in Dutch dog journals. Later D. W. van Brouwershaven did the same. The sporting magazine, *Chasse et Peche,* had an interested editor and carried more than any other publication of the time about the Bouvier. The French, *L'Eleveur,* also carried important Bouvier references. This use of three languages—beyond English—has also made research into Bouvier history difficult.

Huyghebaert stated he drew many of his early historical references from Charles Estienne's *L'Agriculture et Maison Rustique,* first published in Paris in 1564. (Richard Surflet published an English translation in 1600.) Third and succeeding editions, including that from which M. Huyghebaert worked, were co-authored by J. Liebault and J. De Clamorgan and appeared from 1574 on. The author and editor have here amplified some of the points in Miss Bowles' translation.

The word "Bouvier" is French. Many Flemings are bilingual, and especially in the border areas the Flemish and French languages are intermingled. Estienne wrote: "French was spoken especially in regard to all the 'venerie,' hunted animals, horses, cattle and dogs." In Flemish the equivalent of Bouvier would be "Koehond" or "Veedryver."

The Bouvier (Our word, "bovine," describing cattle has the same Latin derivation) was a herdsman who cared for the cows and who also drove the oxcart. Therefore the dog he developed to guard and herd cows became the "Chien de Bouvier" or dog of the herdsman. The sheepdog was called "Chien de Berger" or dog of the sheepherder. The terms have been shortened to Bouvier and Berger.

Some of the Bouvier des Flandres' ancestors became known as

"Pics." For this there are two available explanations. Cattle were raised in Picardie and driven by dogs to the lush Flemish meadows. Thus it could be that because of such commercial relations between the Flanders area and Picardie these dogs became known as Picards, or Pics as a contraction. "Pic," meaning sharp-pointed, or "Picard" for harsh hair offers the alternative explanation. The word, "Bouvier," to describe dogs of this function is not encountered until 18th century writings.

In the Middle Ages "Picards," "Bergeots" and "Matins" were designations the French used for dogs used in driving, guarding and defending cattle. (Marauders included medieval rustlers and dry gulchers—even wild dog packs, lynx, wolves and bears.) The modern Bouvier des Flandres evolved from these dogs.[1] All Belgian working breeds probably trace back to the original Matins which continues as a breed—or type—in Europe. Of course it cannot be presumed today's Matin is the same as the Matin of the Middle Ages. He, too, has evolved through hundreds of dog generations.

It became a practice as far back as the 18th century to cut off the tail and to trim back the ears of guard dogs. Since these appendages were the most vulnerable in encounters with predators they were reduced to near minimums by owners since it was a virtual certainty they would otherwise be lost in encounters far from home and cauterizing materials.[2]

During the early development of the Bouvier it was customary for the head of a household to keep three kinds of dogs. The guard

---

1. Such distinctions might be too finely drawn. A sheepdog and a herding dog might come from a single litter and develop according to each dog's individual talents and the needs of the owners.
2. This is the usual explanation for the docking of ears. There is another, probably much more valid. Drop-eared dogs are prone to infections induced by ear mites which thrive best in warm humid environments. Until very recent times the best available treatment was to trim the ears back so air could circulate within the ear. This reduced the incidence of infection and promoted healing. A third reason for ear triming continues to be the belief by many breeders and owners that prick ears make a dog look more alert, more intimidating and give him "more character." A dog's tail is almost never an object of attack whether the fight is with another dog or with a predator. A tail *is* subject to injury in heavy brush and on a long-haired dog it can become a liability when laden with burrs. A dock-tailed dog loses enough of his balance to slow him a bit. Docking and ear trimming is illegal in some states. Continued practice is probably attributable to owner preference and tradition.

In the Count de Buffon's *Histoire Naturelle* of 1750 this is the way the Chien de Berger was portrayed. In the circa 1825 print below the dog was described both as "le chien de berger" and as "le matin" as if the terms were entirely interchangeable. From the editor's collection.

dog was used to protect life and property against ambushes; the Chien de Berger was used to resist predators and to manage the flock or herd. The third type was a hunting dog.[3]

The dogs destined to guard were large, (truly massive) short of body with great heads and with short, heavy necks. Their muzzles were deep, their jaws powerful. Their eyes were dark and fiery, their ears hairy and sometimes cut. They had wide chests, clublike paws. Tails were short and thick, bespeaking power. Their voices were loud and deep enough to intimidate. They were dark, presumably because they would appear more menacing by day and difficult targets by night. By nature they were ordinarily sedate. They were good watchdogs.

Only torches could provide any significant amount of light outdoors on feudal nights. The realities of the times imposed a curfew. Guard dogs enforced the curfew. By day they were kept penned or tied, often in pairs. They were released after dark to guard the manor or village. This rural police duty was left to the biggest, most powerful dogs, preference being given to those inspiring the most fear because of their appearance.

The lord, the master of the land or "baas" which meant "master" in Flemish, owned at that time, large and small herds of sheep and cattle. Their herding dogs were of many different types. Owners didn't care a great deal about looks, just that the dogs did their jobs well.

Along the two Flanders, from Antwerp to Amsterdam, from Rueben to Brabant, here and there arose a dog different from the common shepherd or sheepdog; different from the cross-breeds that were seen in the cities, and much admired and desired by their owners for their temperament and abilities. These dogs were sought out as sires and reproduced abundantly.

---

3. It appears the true situation has been misinterpreted. During feudal times—and even much later—all of the game belonged to the king or the ruling prince. Some of the highest nobility was permitted to hunt by specific license from the ruler. Penalties for poaching were extremely severe, and the lower the station of the offender, the harsher the penalty. Ownership of a hunting dog was either by royal sufferance or at extreme risk to person and purse. Cowherds were, themselves, bound to the lord and manor in feudal times and can hardly be thought of as "heads of households" as the term is used here. Some emperors, kings and other high nobility had hundreds, even thousands of hunting dogs, and guard dogs suitable for war duties, but cowherds would be fortunate if they could maintain a single dog to help them with their work.

Depicted in a miniature of a 14th century French manuscript are two Matin types wearing spiked collars and fighting wolves. They are massive headed and harsh coated. In all available illustrations early guard dogs resembled the Matins with their overall appearance of roughness with emphasis on bulk and wiry coat.

The sheep dog of this area was not as large nor as massive as the guard dog, but it was a strong, robust animal capable of speed and was used to fight and pursue wolves. People had great fear of wolves at that time and this fear was made worse by the tales told about them. The sheep dog was generally bred to be white so that it could be distinguished from the wolves, and in the belief that it would not frighten the sheep as easily.

With the Matin as the forerunner of the Bouvier, and the "Berger", it should be pointed out that not all Matins had harsh coats. Some were short coated while others had long coats. Dogs tending sheep as well as dogs accompanying ox-drivers or cattle herdsmen varied in outward appearance. Their basic skeletons were rather uniform. Bouvier heads can be recognized in paintings dating as far back as 1827.

A dog with certain Bouvier characteristics is seen in a very rare work by the artist Henry Barnard Chalen who dedicated a series of six lithographs on "The Passions of the Horse" to England's George the Fourth. In plate number four title "Affection" is a dog very much

Guyot's 1867 book described this as "Le chien du berger, petite race"—which can be translated as small type shepherd's dog. There is little difference between this and Buffon's Chien du Berger of 1750. From the editor's collection.

like that described by "Ouida" in her story of 1907, "A Dog of Flanders". It therefore seems possible that dogs evolved or changed little during this time. Chalen's dog has the erect standing small ears of a Bouvier, probably natural rather than cosmetic, a head with the Bouvier's shallow stop, but not the coat of the breed as we know it today. He is of correct size, and while more or less sleek-coated, his thick tail is feathered and he has the bone and substance of a guard dog rather than that of the hunting or racing dog. This dog seems a Bouvier ancestral type.

In the book "Les Races de Chiens" of 1894, a collection of articles previously published by Professor Reul in a veterinary journal and widely accepted during the 1890's as a standard reference on dogs, pleaded the case of the "Belgian Sheepdog" and mentioned the Bouvier. Professor Reul said of the Bouvier, "The cattle dog is for the most part a shepherd dog, or a dog that resembles him in general make-up, but who is bigger, fiercer, more aggressive and has a bolder look."

It is possible to study the works of Flemish painters in the Royal Museum in Antwerp, Belgium. One by Carl Roethard (circa 1650) depicts bear hunting and fighting with a variety of dogs. One type is a rusty brown, harsh-coated dog. Similar dogs are often found in hunting scenes by P. P. Rubens, Jan Fyt, Frans Snyders and Paul Devon. A close relationship between them, the sheep dog and the Bouvier can be seen in Jan Fyt's painting, of "Hunting the Wild Boars" in the Brussels Museum. Fyt lived 1611–1661. Some of these were rough-coated, biting hounds and sheep dogs. The rest closely resembled Bouviers. They were used by noblemen for hunting, and by butchers and other businessmen as guardians of property.

The Dutch painter, Paulus Potter (1625–1654) also painted crossbred Matins and sheep dogs from which it is thought the Bouvier evolved in primitive form. Potter also depicted one of these dogs, chained to a rustic kennel. It appears to be half Greyhound and half sheepdog.

It is sometimes suggested the Matin was crossed to the Scottish Greyhound to gain an even harsher coat for the guard dogs and Matins. The term "Greyhound" was used at that time to describe all sight hunting dogs and the large Scottish Deerhound was used rather than the Russian Wolfhound (Borzoi) or the Greyhound.

Artist Ealaisse who did many of the illustrations for Guyot's *Le Chien* in 1867 might have entitled this "The Discreet Beggars." The dogs are described by name and breed. At left is Polisson, a variety of the Brie shepherds' dog. Charmante is a "chienne de Brie"—a Brie bitch. From the editor's collection.

All varieties of dogs, including the large and small harsh-coated Otterhounds (of which no purebred specimen remains in Belgium), and the harsh- and rough-coated Barbet, (or in Flemish, *Poedelhonden* . . . poodle) had places in early domains. Greyhounds were used to pursue and attack game and predators. Barbets pursued and retrieved anything found in the country, rivers and ponds.

Characteristics of dogs chosen for the hunt are shown in a painting by Carl Roethard where one of the larger, short-bodied, big-headed Matins is taking part in a mythological hunt, "Atalande et Meleagre." This painting, in the Royal Museum at Antwerp, is also called "Chase de Calydon". Roethard depicted a powerful Bouvier type, although the coat and expression is reminiscent of the Briard. This painting suggests the Briard and Bouvier had similar ancestors. This will be explored further on.

It has been surmised that the harsh texture of Bouvier coats may have come from a Matin—Scottish Deerhound cross. It must also be understood that even though dogs were bred for specific purposes there must have been many unplanned crossings due to the crowded, informal kenneling.

While these dogs flourished for centuries in Flemish and French Flanders, in the hunting houses of the Duke of Brabant at Boitsfort and in the forest of Soignes, near Brussels, they spread no farther until much later.

In Flanders the monks of the numerous abbeys crossed the Matins with the Scottish Deerhounds and developed the Bouvier. These abbeys were mostly in desolate and lonely places where powerful, trustworthy guard dogs were needed.

It is generally accepted that the monks of St. Hubert in the Ardennes developed the Bloodhound and the Cisterciens or St. Bernards in the Alps of Switzerland, developed the St. Bernard and gave their names to their breeds. If the Bouvier does not have a patron Saint it may be because he played such a democratic role. Nevertheless, the first breeders of the Bouviers were the monks who founded the powerful Abbey of Duynen on the west coast of Flanders near Coxyde.

The honorary archivist of the town of Furnes, a lawyer named P. de Grave, gives the following information:

> The Abbey of Duynen was founded in 1107. The original buildings were destroyed by the Gueux, heretics of 1566, and later again by the Calvinists in 1577. They were demolished again in 1590 and again in 1593 after which the monks left the region only to return in 1601. This time they settled on the Bogaerts farm, parts of which are still in existence. One turret records a date of reconstruction as 1612.

Over the gates of the dwellings is displayed the coat of arms, and these gates are situated next to what may be the oldest kennel still in existence.

The farm was vast, at least 20,000 acres, and the monks exported significant parts of their crops to England. In 1237 King Henry III authorized the Abbey of Duynen to build wharfs, a fact which offers an insight into the size of the monks' commerce with England. It's probable this maritime commerce dates the monks' importation of Scottish Deerhounds and other breeds of dogs.[4]

---

4. It is just as possible that the dog used was the Irish Wolfhound, a favorite diplomatic gift of English kings.

This is the dog described by Guyot in 1867 as "Chien de Berger (grande race.) He apparently felt there were two distinct size variations, small and large. From the editor's collection.

The Dukes of Burgundy were also importing English dogs, usually hunting dogs. It is a rather ancient custom for royalty and men of rank and importance to exchange gifts of dogs.[5] High clergy had privileges often denied nobility. The Abbot of Duynen must have hunted his own vast forests as well as those of his peers in the hierarchy—as at the Abbey of St. Hubert in the Ardennes.

In an 18th century exchange of letters the Abbot of St. Hubert advised French King Louis XV to import Greyhounds from England to infuse into the St. Hubert Hounds. The Greyhound-Matin cross was more regional. No record is known of Belgian breeds being sent to England but such exports were almost certainly made. If they left any lasting imprint on the British breeds documentation is lacking. Certainly French breeds, strains and types were exploited by English breeders.

Not far from the ancient Duynen site the Bogaerts farm still stands completely surrounded by walls. There is a sort of watchtower, and a kennel which has been reliably dated as 13th century.

A bulletin of the Historical and Archeological Society of Ghent in 1904 indicating the proportions, architectual lines and material undoubtedly prove the age of this kennel as the thirteenth century.

In Flemish, the archway spanning this wall is called "moeffen"

---

5. Lafayette presented George Washington with fine hounds which, in part, helped to found the modern American Foxhound.

which means "cover". There is a gable inside and outside which is of interest archeologically and is also of utilitarian value. Inside this sort of fortification there were some slits through which the watch and guard dogs could scent hear and see to give the alarm to other dogs and to the monks. The sentry dogs could climb the slanting sides of the kennel to get on the top of the wide wall. The wear on the hard stone caused by the heavy chains with which the dogs were tied indicates these must have been powerful and watchful dogs. This was a job to which a dog like the Bouvier-type dog was well suited.

The French artists Desportes (1661–1743) and J. B. Oudry (1686–1755) painted many dogs. The latter was commissioned by Louis XV to immortalize hunts in which the king and his court ladies indulged, some with their Bichon lap dogs. Oudry illustrated the *"Fables of Fontaine"* in which the animals speak by action and expression and for which he was nicknamed "La Fontaine."[6] Oudry, painter to the king, was a careful and appreciative student of nature. He was professor at the Royal School of Painting and was commissioned to design the famous tapestries of Beauvais and Gobelins. Dogs painted by Oudry were authentic portraits. A favorite subject was the Matin, known ancestor of the Bouvier. Of the two Matin types, one was a smooth-coated dog with cropped ears, the other a rough-coated dog with hanging ears. Both types are depicted with spiked collars. Oudry depicts a dog with a smooth coat and thin tail killing a wolf that had attacked a defenseless peasant mother and child. Not true to life, but dramatic. Another Oudry painting depicts a rough-coated dog with a broad skull and short, smooth muzzle. It has a big shaggy tail which could come from a Briard cross. This dog could be an intermediary breeding of the Mastiff and the Bouvier or "Picards" from the French or Flemish Flanders and neighboring countries. Oudry dogs show both Matin and Briard heads. The differences in shape and coat can be clearly seen.

In Flanders, especially around Courtrai, the bleaching of flax for Flemish spinning mills was a most important industry. An advantage was the purity of the waters in the La Lys river and its surrounding meadows. The products of these mills not only appeared on the tables of the rich, but the townships offered them to dukes, clergy, and other people of importance. There are 17th century chronicles of the mayor

---

6. The Fables of La Fontaine is a French version, in poetry, of Aesops Fables.

of Courtrai presenting seventeen pairs of Damask linen tablecloths to King Albert and Isabella when they entered Courtrai on February 3, 1600. A good dog was necessary to guard valuable products such as these.

Dogs of the times also had less noble tasks such as smuggling goods. Guardians or smugglers, the dogs were much like the Bouvier and the heavy-coated Briard. The Briard originated east of Paris in the French region of "de Brie". Similar dogs were found in Belgium.

An accurate description of the Briard was given by Professor Reul in 1891, the year of the first dog show. He described them as being more or less pure silver grey with a blue tinge, double dew claws and very alert. Pierre Megnin, father of the director of "L'Eleveur", in Paris, described the Briard as a cross of the "chien de Berger" or "Beauce" or short coated sheepdog and the Barbet, or water dog.

Measurements of the Briard and the "Beauce" are generally the same. Many fanciers consider Briards to be of Belgian origin because they were there for so long.

At an exhibit in 1876 the French painter, Leon Hermann, was lauded for his painting of a shepherd near the sea with his two dogs.

An etching after Leon Hermann by C. W. Coutry indicates the artist did more than one painting on the shepherd dog theme. The dogs depicted in his "Evening Star" are either Bouviers, or Bouvier ancestoral types. The engraving was published Jan. 1, 1868 by A. Delorus, 68 rue J.J. Rousseau. From the Horowitz collection.

In the foreground is a long-haired dog lying quietly at the shepherd's feet and looking straight ahead. It is undoubtably a Briard type. The other dog, harsh-coated with a Bouvier head, stands intently watching a flock of grazing sheep.

The geographical location of Picardie, home of the Briard and its forerunner the Picard, next to Flanders on one side and the sea on the other, lent itself to the easy crossing, and the development of the Bouvier. This area was well known for its horses and cattle, which increased the demand for powerful dogs on the farms. They were needed to furnish power for spinning mills and for churns. They gave customs officials "muscle" and pulled carts among other duties.

Documentation of the Bouvier origin is fragmentary. Most of the information from this point has come from a French director of customs who had been contacted by the late F. E. Verbanck, a famed

This photo of Fram from *Chasse et Pêche* via De Bylandt's 1905 *Dogs of All Nations* is proof that at the turn of the century there were Bouviers that could conform rather well to today's standards for the Bouvier des Flandres. Fram was owned by J. Jochmann of Utrecht. From the editor's collection.

breeder of Bouviers from Ghent. In letters the officer stated many records were lost during World War I. All that was found was a report of a sheepdog (Berger) and a Griffon mix and its accomplishments in about six years of service with the customs department. During this period the dog, working with its officer-master, captured about four hundred dogs being used by smugglers, many with merchandise on their backs, going alone or lying low in the woods. This dog discovered many hiding places for smuggled goods and inspired fear in the smugglers. He was described as a massive, powerful dog. In 1902 and 1903 this same dog obtained several prizes at the shows of Roubaix and Lille, but his name has not been successfully researched.

The name "berger-griffon" used to describe this dog may seem peculiar to many people but it was appropriate in terms of Bouvier evolution at the turn of the century.

Under the name of "Griffon," which in France is used for a hunting dog with a harsh coat and a large amount of Barbet or water dog blood, dogs were crossed for twenty years with sheepdogs and Picards. Confirmation of these crossings comes from an 1899 report by the well-known Dutch Griffon breeder, G. F. Leliman.

According to German authors, the Barbet or waterdog, was obtained by crossing a long haired sheep dog with a medium sized hunting dog, or "Treibhund". Leliman draws attention to the first pedigreed harsh-

From the "atlas" to Guyot's *Le Chien,* Paris, 1867, comes this engraving of "Les griffons d'arret francais"—literaly rough-coated French dogs of stop— or rough-coated French pointing dogs. A cobby body type would have to come from another source but the coat is inescapably similar to that of the Bouvier. From the editor's collection.

coated hunting dogs raised in Germany by the Dutchman, E. K. Korthals, which were shown in Frankfort in 1878. "But," says Leliman, "These dogs, Moustach I, Lina, Querida and Tampa, were French, as the catalog class name 'Griffons a Poil due'[7] indicated. However, these dogs of Korthals came from Holland, Germany and probably Belgium and France. In Holland, even now in the Drenthe, there are Griffons exactly the type of 'Mouche,' Korthals' first bitch, who was

7. An enthusiastic but erroneous conclusion, this illustrates how easy it is for breed histories to drift into fiction.

A Dutch herding dog, Trotteur, posed with his owner, J. Westerwoudt of Baarn for this turn of the century photo. Reprinted from *Hondenrassen*, a two-volume dog encyclopedia by L. Seegers, published in Amsterdam, 1912. From the Gerace collection.

one of the seven purebreds of 'Imperwoud'. They could just as well have originated in Hesse or Bruswick . . . their origin is unknown."

If writers of all nationalities are unable to give precise origin to the Griffons of Korthals, or Korthals Griffons as they are known today,[8] it is no wonder they can do no better for the Bouviers.

Like needs and climates can produce very similar dog breeds. When this phenomenon occurs in nature scientists call it parallel but separate development. In virtually every European country there have existed for centuries sheepdogs with long, harsh hair. Any or several of these could have been ancestors of the Belgian (small letter) bouvier. Wars and commerce brought many nationalities to and through Belgian and French Flanders and Dutch Zeeland. Herding dogs which might have been called Bouviers might have been introduced from Roulers or from Ardennes. Even Riezenschnauzers (Giant Schnauzers) from the mountainous country to the west might have made genetic contributions. To assign frontiers to the Bouvier is impossible.

Belgians have been successful, creative breeders for many centuries. Their horses and other livestock give ample testimony to their skills. In dogs they seem to have particular talents for breeding, selecting and training.

Early in the 20th century two Flemish breeders near La Lys, Paret and Moerman, deliberately set out to purify the Belgian bouvier. They, and other breeders, used sheepdogs, Matins and mixed breeds.

8. In the U.S. they are known as Wirehaired Pointing Griffons.

Belgian customs officers with their dogs, about 1900. Photo reproduced from Toepoel's *Honden Encyclopaedia*. Those at left and right seem to be Bouvier types. From the editor's collection.

This is recorded in the catalog of the St. Hubert Club of the North (France) for the fourth international show held at Roubaux in 1905. Depicted on the cover is a customs officer leading a muzzled sheepdog. Only working dogs listed in the control books of the customs officers were eligible for showing.

Of the 43 dogs entered, 14 were short-coated. Here's the way the ten males in Open Class 237 were listed and described:[9]

441	Cartouche	brindle, white on chest, whelped 8/6/1903 out of Coco.
442	Marquis	russet fawn, June 1900, out of Turc and Sophie
443	Garcon	Black, white chest, april 21, 1902 out of Gros and Lisette
444	Mousse	light gray, April 1904, out of Tuc and Marquise
445	Finard	steel gray, April 1904
445	Picard	gray brindle, long hair on back and muzzle. July 16, 1903, out of Picard and Comtesse
447	Matelet	April 10, 1903
448	Brutus	brindle, March 1904
449	Compagnon	fawn, 5½ years old out of Turc and Lisette
450	Turc	Steel gray, white chest, April 1903 out of Leon and Lisette

Open Class #238 included these six females:

| 451 | Marquise | steel gray, 9 years old, Prize of honor taken at Lille 1904 |
| 452 | Diana | dark chestnut, 9 years old, out of Turc and Diane |

9. Historian Huyghebaert noted he was unable to reconcile sires, dams and dates of these entries—as given. There are two possible explanations, both of which may be valid. Early registrations were often based upon recollection rather than records. Also, geographical areas often use favorite names for dogs. (In the U.S. these have been Rex, Prince, King and Queenie.) For example, the Lisette that whelped Compagon in 1899 might have been quite another Lisette than the entered bitch of the same name showing a whelping date of 1901.

453	Mirza	Reddish black, white chest Feb. 1904 (See 1912 photo.)
454	Lisette	gray brindle, black muzzle, Oct. 1901, out of Baron and Lionne
455	Blanche	gray muzzle with black hair, white feet, May 14, 1902 Silver medal of the Club St. Hubert.
456	Mandat	gray brindle, Dec. 1901, out of Brutus and Fatma.

Unfortunately no good photograph has been found of the entered Picard,[10] with his silver-gray, long harsh coat on his back and muzzle. His sire, also Picard, was probably one of the unknown ancestors of the Bouviers in the Paret and Moerman family. All these dogs had crosses of the sheepdog and Matin in them. Later, even after the creation of pedigrees and the Book of Origins (LOSH), in litters from "purebred" parents there were puppies similar to these harsh-coated crossbreds.

At first, and for apparent good reasons, pups with obvious faults such as spots on chests and feet were eliminated so as not to mar the reputation of their litter-mates. Some breeders, however, realized that in doing this they were also destroying some very good qualities which were needed.

In his 1905 *Dogs of All Nations* Count Henri DeBylandt noted that there were French and Belgian types of the "Chien Bouvier." Even at that early date he treated them as distinct from the "Chien de Brie" or Briard. Here are the points of the breed as he published them at the turn of the century in the same year during which the first Bouvier competition took place.

Chien de Bouvier
FRENCH CATTLE DOG.

General appearance. A strong dog, with a somewhat savage appearance, well coated with rough and hard hair. **Head.** Well made,

---

10. See the 1912 photo of the Bouviers exhibited at Brussels in June, 1912. The Mirza at that show may, or may not, be the same Mirza in the first recorded, 1905, Bouvier exhibition. She would have been, if the same, nine years old at Brussels. She probably is not the Mirza appearing in Betty de la Lys' pedigree on a subsequent page in this chapter. That Mirza shows a different owner—although she could have been sold. Show-minded enthusiasts were aggressively buying breeding stock during that period. Ed.

longish; muzzle not too short; skull broad and rounded. **Eyes.** Rather small, piercing and intelligent; colour dark brown. **Nose.** Always black. **Ears.** Erect and small. **Teeth.** Very strong and meeting evenly. **Neck.** Strong and well muscled. **Body.** Well built, strong and elegant. **Legs.** Well boned, straight and muscular. **Feet.** Strong. **Tail.** Bushy, of medium length; carried upwards but not over the back. **Coat.** Rather long and of a good hard texture, sometimes shorter, but profusely coated all over. **Colour.** Black, dark tawny, or a black saddle and dirty brown on legs, belly and underside of tail. **Height at shoulder.** From $25\frac{1}{2}$ to $29\frac{1}{2}$ inches. **Weight.** From 65 to 75 lb.

Monsieur Paret, the Bouvier fancier of Ghent, is justly considered to have established the foundation bloodlines of our present day Bouviers. In 1943 Mr. L. Huyghebaert wrote:

> I have had the personal pleasure to judge the sire Rex (RSH 1766) and the dam Nelly (RSH 1892), both shown at the International in Brussels on May 21-23, 1910, at the Cinquantenaire Park, organized by the Societe Royal Saint Hubert. The Bouviers are only represented by two dogs. I rejoice to see this breed represented by so few. The Bouviers are not show dogs and will not gain by shows when one sees what happens to native breeds. I only hope they will stay away from shows as long as possible. I remember the humiliating asterisk still placed next to the variety of Bouviers in the official catalogues (1927) of the new indigenous sheepdogs—being of too lowly origin to find a place in the stud books—and these were the 'gothas' of dogs. Since then our sheepdogs have found a place and different types are now recognized. Certainly these are fine results, but alas, how many poor ones as to character and temperament are to be found in the shows? Let this be a lesson to Bouvier fanciers. If they are bent to show let there be no exaggerations and retain the true character of the breed and type of the breed. The temperament is excellent. Just look at the eye of Rex and Nelly. Rex is by far the better of the two—he is more typey. Nelly has more of the Sheepdog expression. As I have said at the show in Amsterdam in 1909, I repeat; the Bouvier should look gruff and rustic—he should be a block, not something elegant. I do not know whether I was right. The fact is in 1910 the Bouviers and different types of sheepdogs were not well-defined yet, but it is due to the perserverance of L. Paret with the good councils of the editor of *Chasse et Peche,* that finally the Bouviers became taken seriously. A French magazine, *L'Eleveur* drew the

attention of foreign fanciers and specializing clubs became interested."

After 1910 two tendencies were seen. The small Bouviers with natural standing ears and short tail were called, for awhile, "bergeot" by the Walloons of the Wallonie district and later called the Bouvier d'Ardennes. Concurrently with this small Bouvier, there was a larger Bouvier, one having more Matin blood. This one immediately became the more popular and also became known by different names: Bouvier de Roulers, Belgian Bouvier, or French Bouvier of Flandres.

The Bouvier d'Ardennes might as well be called the little Bouvier. He is an intermediary between the sheepdog which is relatively longer and the cobby Matin-type Bouvier. The Bouvier d'Ardennes' naturally standing uncropped ears mark him unlike other Bouviers. This characteristic suggests a closer relationship to the harsh-coated sheepdog. It was thought at the time that this Bouvier would prevail and become better known in the area for its grand cattle-driving and cart-pulling abilities.

A description of the Bouvier d'Ardennes appeared in the 1947 book, *Working Dogs of the World* by Clifford L. B. Hubbard:

> The head is moderate in breadth, and of fair length with little stop. The eyes are dark and medium in size; the ears rather small and erect. The body is rather square with a strong level back, deep chest and muscular loins. The legs are of medium length and rather heavy in bone, with round medium feet; the tail is of full natural length, set low and carried low to the hocks, usually with

A Bouvier d'Ardennes of 1913. Reproduced from Toepoel's *Honden Encyclopaedia*. From the editor's collection.

Boer-Sus was described as a Belgian Sheepdog in *Chasse et Pêche* and Count Henri de Bylandt's *Dogs of All Nations,* 1905. The owner was Hautôt of Brussels. From the editor's collection.

a slight final curl upward. The coat is fairly short on the head and legs, and medium on the neck, flanks, back and hindquarters, and dense, rough and shaggy. The colours vary from all black to light gray, with the darker grays flecked with black and being fairly common. Light brindles and grays with white points are also occasionally found. The height is generally about 22 inches.

The year 1910 was an unfavorable time for the development of cattle dogs and other farm dogs. These dogs were no longer a necessity as the townpeople were following the fashions. A revival was seen for police dog usage, and sought was a larger, heavier dog which would inspire more respect. The Bouvier d'Ardennes was superceded by the Bouvier de Roulers which was more massive and whose height was 27½ inches. It was accepted in a meeting held in Roulers in 1912. Here is an extract from an article published in 1912 and written by Vital Taeymans:

> The Roeselaersche Hondenclub has decided to study and discuss the propositions of the veterinarian, Dr. Louis Schaerlaeken, S.R.S.H. delegate, concerning the characteristics of the Bouviers called 'Picard'. Those present were Messrs. A. Houtard, J. Levita,

Un groupe de Bouviers des Flandres à l'Exposition de Juin 1912 du Kennel Club belge Bruxelles.

1 Martin d'Ypres
2 Lucien de Lille
3 Dominant Isenheim
4 Deltuck Ypres
5 7 Dubois Lille
6 Lepoivre d'Ypres
7 & 8 : L'amateur de Lille

a : Maarten de Warnant M.
b : Gié d'Hazennes M.
c : Jyva de Louvain M.
d : Nicke Lepoivre Duisburg F
e : Spot de Val Duchesse M

f : Draine d'Hultremeulen F elle
g : Dick de Bourcinque M
h : Mirza E à Molenaine
i : Olga de Triste à semple (elle)

An historic moment in the development of the modern Bouvier is captured in this photo of the Bouvier exhibitors and their dogs at the 1912 Brussels show. The key to identifications is reproduced on the page opposite. Photo lent by Club National Belge du Bouvier des Flandres.

Baron J. Van Zuylen van Nyeveld of the S.R.S.H., and Messrs Orban and Taeymans as judges. After having examined the best representatives of the breed, a standard was adopted. Here follows a resume of these examinations: **General appearance:** rustic and imposing **Ears:** cropped and carried erect **Chest:** deep but not too wide **Trunk and back:** short, robust and straight (like a cob horse) **Colors:** Black, slate grey, brown, etc.

In an article published and titled *To Whom the Future,* Vital Taeymans concluded it would be with the Picards that the breed would evolve as they were larger, more calm and steady than the sheepdogs. Large dogs were most in demand. Taeymans, an administrator of the S.R.S.H., would be authoritative as to what the majority of the then-breeders wanted. And, the breeders catered to the general demand.

In 1912, M. F. Fontaine, vice president of the Club St. Hubert of the North was trying to push a smaller Bouvier under the name of Bouvier des Flandres against the Bouvier de Roulers. In France, M. Fontaine was considered a specialist and here follows his opinion: In *Chasse et Peche* of April 6, 1912 he wrote:

> In the north of France around Warneton and Ypres near the frontier, there exists a harsh-coated dog used by shepherds. This is the Bouvier des Flandres that resembles a 'Berger Picard', a product seemingly of a cross with a Matin.
>
> The Matin cross has increased size. The Berger Picard is medium size with a maximum height of $23\frac{5}{8}$ inches and the Bouvier would be $25\frac{1}{2}$ inches. I have noticed this the last fifteen years in the farm dogs as I have judged around Lille. The color of these Picard sheepdogs is black interspersed with white hairs, or dark brindle.
>
> In these agricultural shows I have also seen some Bouviers, but they were fewer, all entered in classes called 'Sheepdogs and Bouvier.' I have given an extra prize to these Bouviers to extend deserved distinction and to encourage their promotion.

This excerpt was followed by the standard, illustrated by the head of a Bouvier des Flandres with natural standing ears. The description, except for size, was about the same as for the Bouvier des Roulers. Size was set at $23\frac{5}{8}$ to $25\frac{1}{2}$ inches for males, and $22\frac{3}{4}$ to $24\frac{1}{2}$ inches for females.

The Bouvier des Roulers description given by Fontaine is that of a farm and guard dog. Beyond being a herder of cattle, oxen and cows, he is listed a merchant's guard dog, a dog for defense and draught. On the farm he is also used to power the churn.

Ranked by size there was, first, the harsh-coated sheep dogs at 21½ to 23⅝ inches, the Bouvier des Flandres at 23⅝ to 25½ inches and, last, the giant Bouvier de Roulers at 25½ to 27½ inches. From these three the modern Bouvier is evolved.

The best dogs at that time, and which were most used as progenitors and recorded in the Stud Book were Champion Nic de Sottegem (LOSH 10766), Dragon de la Lys (LOSH 11776) Milton (LOSH 15936), and Goliath de la Lys (LOSH 11736). Nic and Milton are of unknown origin. During the war, in 1917, Nic was bought on a farm and taken home. Of Milton, only his sire, Brick, and his dam Lize, are known.

In 1921 the Bouvier Club de Courtrai which was affiliated with the Kennel Club Belge convened and decided that unquestionably there were two types of Bouviers. One was small, usually grey or fawn and light colored, (never black) short ribbed and with a fairly short head. Its ears were cut and its tail was docked. It was most predominently found on the farms and grazing regions situated between the La Lys river and the north seacoast. The variety was known as the Paret type after L. Paret's Rex and Nelly. It was more the shepherd type then, but has evolved into the Bouvier des Flandres. Until the time when the Paret Bouvier came by its name it was also called "vuilbaard" (dirty beard) "Koehond" (Flemish for cow dog), "toucheur de boeuf" or 'chien de vacher" meaning cowherd's dog. The standard the Club de Courtrai applied to the Paret Bouvier des Flandres was called the "Standard Domicent" after Dr. Domicent who led the investigation.

The cowherds and fanciers of the area then established that another type of cow dog "Bouvier" existed and for this type they formed the "Standard Roberfroid," named after its leading protagonist. This dog also had cropped ears and docked tails, but it was larger than the Paret type with a deeper chest, longer head and it was almost always black. Before this historic meeting, it had been referred to as the Moerman, Bouvier Belge, or Bouvier de Roulers.

As might be expected, there was a cross between these two types exemplified by a dog named "Washington Bonaparte" who possessed much of the charm of both the Bouvier des Flandres (Paret) and the Bouvier de Roulers (Moerman).

With these two main types to the front, it is unfortunate that still another cow dog of the area was never given recognition, but actually barred from the shows as undesirable. However, it was a strong type of dog, often black or dark grey with so much hair as to resemble an Old English Sheepdog. It has not, however, disappeared. On the continent it is known as the Bouvier Briarde.[11]

And lastly, but not least, came the dog of the Ardennes that seemed to contribute so much to the beginnings of the modern Bouvier, but who himself remained rather unrecognized.

It was decided at the meeting at Courtrai that the first type, the Bouvier des Flandres, was really the oldest of all the others. This type was mostly fawn or light grey—the genetic source of the fawns of today.

11. Recognized by the AKC as the "Briard."

Here are the three Bouvier types of 1912. Pick de Boesinghe and Mirza (upper left) were representative of the French type. Marius des Baies, (lower left) more massive, was typical of the type favored by Belgian breeders and judges. The debate continued until 1961. A 1912 intermediate type was the fawn Washington Bonaparte (below). Photos reproduced from *L'Elevage*, official monthly of the Kennel Club Belge.

The second type they decided was "manufactured" by taking the first and crossing it with the Matin, but that this "de Roulers" type, while bigger, stronger and always black, was not atypical and would not survive. Therefore two standards were drawn up for these two main types of Bouviers and it was decided that only the future could tell which would survive. The Bouvier Club de Courtrai at this point should have listened to the sage advise of one modest counsellor. He said: "The two varieties will have to be used in forming a single breed since one will be in need of the other if they are to survive at all." However, two Bouvier standards still existed in Belgium. The Bouvier des Flandres is recognized by the American Kennel Club. The Bouvier de Roulers is not.

Not once but twice the Bouvier was nearly exterminated by world wars waged upon his breeding grounds. Only because he served his masters so well and so loyally was the Bouvier able to survive in a few hard-core breeding strongholds in France, Belgium and Holland.

In 1918 the Bouvier made a comeback. A few families had managed to keep their dogs through the war. Sultan, belonging to Mr. Van der Vennet and to Mr. Gryson, and Picko belonging to Mr. De Poorter, and two other notable dogs, Bella and Kiss de Ramillies, escaped and left progeny leading to today's Bouviers. The one dog that did most to revive the Bouvier in Belgium lived with veterinary Army Captain Darby and was Nic de Sottegem. Nic became a champion of Belgium and was shown at the Olympic show at Antwerp in 1920. The judge, Charles Huge, wrote: "Nic is the ideal type of the Bouvier. He has a short body, with well developed ribs, short flanks, strong legs,

Champion Nic de Sottegem, LOSH 10766, was the great progenitor of the modern Bouvier des Flanders. He was on the scene in the post-World War I era when a great sire was needed. Virtually every great Bouvier of today of predominately Belgian breeding traces back to Nic through several lines. This rare photograph reproduced from Toepoel's *Honden Encyclopaedia*. From the editor's collection.

Dragon de la Lys and his kennelmate, Goliath de la Lys, both sired by Ch. Nic de Sottegem, were worthy successors to their sire during the late 20's and early 30's. This rare photo of Dragon de la Lys is also from Toepoel's *Honden Encyclopaedia*. From the editor's collection.

good feet, long and oblique shoulders. His head is of a good shape with somber eyes and an ideal courageous expression. His hair is dry and dark. The tail should not have been cut so short. I hope that the dog will have numerous progeny."

Charles Huge's wishes were realized, for when Nic died in 1926 he left a great many descendants among which we might note Prince D'or, Ch. Draga Coralie de Sottegem, Goliath de la Lys, Lyda Nefte de la Paix, Nora, Siske de Sottegem and Ch. Dragon de la Lys.

Of the early kennels the most prominent was "de la Lys". The owner, M. Gryson of St. Denis Westrem, did not hesitate to use the best he could find. His best dogs were Dragon de la Lys and Goliath de la Lys, both, as noted, sired by Champion Nic.

Many of these dogs figure in the pedigree of Actif, LOSH 16357, the top-rated dog of 1924. Here's that pedigree:

```
                                    Ch. Nic de Sottegem, LOSH 10766   Unknown
                                                                      Unknown
                          Nicolo de la Lys, LOSH 11712, grey
                                    Margot                            Pickzwart, LOSH 14959
                                                                      Mirza, M. DeBruyne, owner
              Goliath de la Lys, LOSH 11736, grey
                                    Unknown                           Unknown
                                                                      Unknown
                          Flandrienne, LOSH 11736, grey
                                    Cora                              Unknown
                                                                      Unknown
ACTIF, LOSH 16357
                                    Unknown                           Unknown
                                                                      Unknown
                          Ch. Nic de Sottegem, LOSH 10766
                                    Unknown                           Unknown
                                                                      Unknown
              Durca de la Lys
                          Pickzwart, LOSH 14959                       Unknown
                                                                      Unknown
                          Ch. Draga, LOSH 10773, black
                                    Cora                              Unknown
                                                                      Unknown
```

Although the name Dragon de la Lys does not appear in this pedigree one can see the bloodlines. He is a brother, from a previous litter, of Durca de la Lys, dam of Actif.

In early pedigrees the name of Duduc (12872) is often seen. He was a stud used by the breeders of Courtrai and thus he appears in pedigrees of many breeders. A member of this family is Betty de la Lys (11774), kennel mate of Milton (15936), and one of the best bitches of her time. This is her pedigree:

```
                                Unknown                          Unknown
                        Unknown                                  Unknown
                                Unknown                          Unknown
                Ch. Nic de Sottegem, LOSH 10766, black           Unknown
                                Unknown                          Unknown
                        Unknown                                  Unknown
                                Unknown                          Unknown
                                                                 Unknown
BETTY DE LA LYS, LOSH 11774
                                Filou, LOSH 9569, C. Vander Heeren, owner    Pic, Moerman, owner
                        Dudac, LOSH 12872                        Charlotte, Vander Heeren, owner
                                Lize, C. Vander Heeren, owner    Unknown
                Lyda, LOSH 10278, grey                           Unknown
                                Filou, LOSH 9569, C. Vander Heeren, owner    Pic, Moerman, owner
                        Tata                                     Charlotte, Vander Heeren, owner
                                Mirza, M. DeBruyne, owner        Unknown
                                                                 Unknown
```

Here again Champion Nic de Sottegem, of unknown origin, was a producer of top quality.

The Club National Belge du Bouvier des Flandres was organized in January 1921. In July 1923, in Ghent, well-known breeders and judges carefully examined well known Bouviers of that time. From a concensus of their evaluations of these dogs they wrote the official standard of the breed. Those who formulated this more comprehensive Belgian standard were Messrs. Charles Huge, V. Tenret, V. Taeymans, Count de Hemptinne, Captain Binin and A. Gevaert. The dogs they carefully measured and examined were Prince D'or, Ch. Draga de la Lys, Coralie de Sottegem, Goliath de la Lys, Lyda Nefte de la Paix, Nora, Ch. Dragon de la Lys, Ch. Nic de Sottegem, Trotsky, Sultan, Morki, Flandrienne and Blondine. These were the basic post World War I foundation dogs.

The very first special show for Bouviers was in Saint-Denis Westrem in 1925 and was organized by the Club National Belge du Bouvier des Flandres. The twenty-two entries were judged by L. Van Damme. In the class for junior males, first place winner was Cesar de Pont-a-rieu; first place female was Zora de Zwynaerde. In the open class for males, Bouboule, owned by Jules Rassehaert won. The open bitch winner was Molly, owned by M. Patttyn. The judge's report on Boubole read: "Magnificent type in head and expression, good shoulders, well built body and legs, also a good coat and gait—though a little stiff in forelegs." Here is his pedigree:

Bouboule de Cortrai was a winning representative of the de Courtrai kennels, one of the pioneering Bouvier breeding establishments. In 1925 he drew a rave report from Judge L. Van Damme after winning the open male class at the first Bouvier specialty. Photo from Toepoel's *Honden Encyclopaedie*. From the editor's collection.

```
                                    Unknown
               Unknown               Unknown
      Jim de Sellier, LOSH 19345     Unknown
               Unknown               Unknown
  Bobby du Sellier, LOSH 16547       Unknown
               Unknown               Unknown
      Bella du Sellier, Mme Canbien, owner
               Unknown               Unknown
                                     Unknown
BOUBOULE DE CONTRAI (1924)
                                     Unknown
               Unknown               Unknown
      Ch. Nic de Sottegem, LOSH 10766, black
               Unknown               Unknown
  Arga de la Lys                     Unknown
          Pickzwart, LOSH 14959      Unknown
      Riga, LOSH 11754               Unknown
          Flandrienne, LOSH 11736    Cora
```

Nickol recieved many prizes under Judge Charles Huge and Judge Vital Taeymans. Here's his pedigree:

```
                                    Unknown
               Unknown               Unknown
      Pick, M. van Damme, owner      Unknown
               Unknown               Unknown
  Picko                              Unknown
               Unknown               Unknown
      Mira                           Unknown
               Unknown               Unknown

NICKOL, LOSH 17522 (1923)
                                     Pic, Moerman, owner
      Filou, LOSH 9569               Charlotte, Doussy, owner
  Max                                Unknown
      Bitch, M. Van der Venne, owner Unknown
  Belatte                            Unknown
               Unknown               Unknown
      Vara, LOSH 10280               Unknown
          Mirza, M. DeBruyne, owner  Unknown
```

The concensus standard of the 1923 Ghent conference was called the "Standard Gevaert" and was patterned after the "Standard Roberfroid." (Monsieur Roberfroid was instrumental in formulating the Moerman or Bouvier de Roulers standard for the black type). The Societe Royal Saint-Hubert was emerging as predominant in Belgium.

This is the photo Toepoel used to illustrate the "Vlaamsche Koehond of Bouvier" or "Bouvier Belge des Flandres" section in his *Honden Encyclopaedie*. He did not identify the dog but he certainly selected a cobby model with an elegant carriage and stance. From the editor's collection.

It published the "Standard Gevaert"—which differed from the Roberfroid in that it admitted all colors.

Breeding in conformity with these two standards began to produce a most formidable dog. He was very squarely built, with the characteristic massive chest development of true Bouviers. A well-chiseled head was proudly carried on a muscular neck. Becoming fixed as breed trademarks were the eyebrows, mustache and beard. Along with the alert eyes of a guard dog they bespoke the Bouvier's character and expression. The tail, placed highly and gaily carried, gave accent to a personality full of zest, fire and zeal. Four pillar-like and well-boned legs carried him without heaviness in his gait. At this time his tail was docked to about four inches and his ears cropped to a triangular contour.

In 1926, a meeting of the Kennel Club Belge at Boitsfer failed in its mission to unite the two main fractions of the breed and bring the Bouvier under one standard. Things remained the same until the K.C.B. decided to again modify procedure by having dogs judged in two classes according to color. This appeared fine until size and color conflicts were encountered. A light colored dog under the name of Bouvier des Flandres might not be the size that the Bouvier de Roulers standard demanded. A Societe Royal Saint-Hubert Belgian champion could be eliminated from the show ring at the Societe Central of

France as too big. Only size and color divided these variations. Through many debates, arguments and discussions between Belgium and France, the impasse remained. It appeared there might never be agreement.

In 1929 the American Kennel Club recognized the Bouvier des Flandres as a breed. In 1931 the AKC registered two Bouviers—the first on its books. On April 14, 1959 the AKC approved the present standard for the breed.

In 1961 the official Club du Bouvier des Flandres for France Bulletin number seven proclaimed:

> For 40 years the subject of a unified standard for the Bouvier des Flandres has caused floods of ink. Belgian judges going to France and French judges going to Belgium have concluded that there is no more difference in evaluation and that the road is now open for a fusion of the standards.
>
> The Club du Bouvier des Flandres for France and the Club National Belge du Bouvier des Flandres have discussed this problem for two years. Commissions were designated and on March 12, 1961, the French and Belgian commissions assembled and approved the unified standard of the Bouvier des Flandres.
>
> This is a memorable date in the history of the Bouvier des Flandres. We hope we have worked well for the breed.

With one standard adopted by Belgium and France breeders at last had a common ideal toward which they could cooperatively work. The Netherlands has a variation of the Bouvier standard which is quite similar and dogs registered with their National Raad van Beheer as "Bouvier Belge des Flandres" are normally accepted by the AKC for registration in its stud records.

During the 1930's and into the World War II era the general type of the Bouvier was maintained in all three of the breed's native countries, but there were variations on several points. All of the Bouviers had short, harsh coats to a degree but many were longer bodied with lighter bone than desired. In Belgium and France there emerged the type we now think of as the modern Bouvier—longer coated and cobbier. Dutch breeders have more recently followed the trend. They have used strong infusions of Belgian stock and produce first class dogs.

It was once common to refer to Bouviers with harsh, short coats as the "Dutch type." At one time all Bouviers were clothed

Fricko de Belgique dramatically illustrates the shortness of body and the sense an power and alertness which are distinctive to the Bouvier. Fricko, by Arian out of Donatienne des Coudreaux is prominent in many Belgian and American pedigrees.

with fairly short, harsh coats—and without the undercoat which is a firmly-fixed breed characteristic today. Variations are still sometimes detectable in the Bouviers exported to the U.S. from the Netherlands. Some breeders advocate keeping the two types separate, but since both are registered as Bouviers des Flandres it is the author's opinion that with good judgement in breeding and discrimination in culling, the two types will merge to the benefit of both.

THE BOUVIER COMES TO AMERICA

THERE is probably no record of the first Bouvier imported into the the United States. The probability is that it was brought here by an emigrant family wanting a bit of its native Flanders with it in America.

There appears some mystery about the AKC's "recognition" of the Bouvier. The mystery seems to arise from attempting to understand the American Kennel Club's actions in the 1920's in the light of that body's present day procedures. Much of the terminology remains the same but concept and procedure have had some revolutionary changes.

The AKC's records indicate the Bouvier became eligible for registration in 1926. Other records show formal "recognition" in 1929. The first edition of the AKC's official *The Complete Dog Book* in 1929 had a chapter on the Bouvier with the standard of the Club National du Bouvier des Flandres—and a full page photo.

It must be assumed Americans were importing Bouviers throughout the twenties. Soldiers in foreign lands have historically brought native breeds of dogs home with them. Tens of thousands of World War II doughboys must have been exposed to Bouviers as they fought across Flanders.

Whatever the dates of the Bouviers first AKC admissability and recognition, it was not until the May, 1931 *Stud Book* that the first Bouviers were officially recorded in the U.S. There were two and both were imported by George MacCullough Miller of Old Westbury, New York.

The dogs, both grizzles, were full brother and sister from different litters. The first, AKC 780160, was Hardix (LOSH 34814), whelped Nov. 20, 1926. He was bred by Tabellion and Gand at Rue Alexis Pesnon 46, Montreuil, Seine, France. Diane de Montreuil, AKC 780161, whelped May 30, 1927, was bred by Marette and Gand.

For whatever reasons there were no further Bouvier registrations with the AKC until a single entry in 1935. Thus it appears that through the first ten years of AKC eligibility Hardix and Diane de Montreuil were the only Bouviers recorded. Popular breeds in that era were Boston Terriers, German Shepherds and Airedales. Boxers and Briards were doing little better in the United States than was the Bouvier.

The pedigree of Hardix and Diane followed classic patterns:

              Ch. Nic de Sottegem
      Dragon de la Lys
              Draga
  Lutin de Mouscron
              Piston
      Sarah de Sottegem
              Coralie

Hardix (AKC 780160) 11/20/26 and Diane de Montreuil (AKC 780161) 5/30/27

              Goliath de la Lys
      Azur
              Durca de la Lys
  Zette du Roy d'Espange
              Duc
      Blondine
              Diane

An early importer was Louis de Rochemont of New York. From The Netherlands he brought Czardas van Het Bunderbosch. Czardas, whelped in 1938, was bred by M. Widdershoven of Bunde. Imported in 1936 was Coba uit het Zuiderlicht (NHSB 25619). Whelped in 1932, she was also bred in The Netherlands by J. J. H. Klinkers. Her sire's great-grand dam was the famed foundation bitch, Flandrienne. Pedigrees of imports from The Netherlands generally reveal that

THE FIRST BOUVIER REGISTERED BY THE AKC? This is the photo which illustrated the Bouvier in the AKC's official *The Complete Dog Book* from its earliest 1929 edition until the most recent in 1972. The AKC does not identify its breed models. One report, via an early U.S. Bouvier breeder, states this is a portrait of Hardix, the first Bouvier registered by the AKC. There appears to be no way this report can be checked. Although Hardix wasn't registered until 1931 the import was whelped in 1926. He could have been mature enough in 1928 or 1929 to have posed for this picture. The new AKC model is the now-retired Ch. Naris du Posty Arlequin. The AKC book's photo of the all-time show record holder among Bouviers is the same used as the frontispiece of this book.

the Dutch used many of the same foundation dogs that served the Belgians and French so well.

Will Judy in his *Dog Encyclopedia* remarked that it was very strange the AKC chose to recognize the Bouvier for exhibition and show purposes as the breed was seldom seen in America. He pointed out however that it was simply a matter of a majority vote in a quorum of AKC directors—in this instance four favorable directors.

During the Bouvier's early years in the U.S. Julius Bliss was the man who kept things going. He provided the communication and the stimulus for breeders and owners. He promoted the breed unselfishly, he showed and until his untimely death, imported excellent stock. He bred his imported Laraine to George Young's Bojar van

Bouvier history is captured in this photograph. At the left is Belco. When the Nazis put a price on her head Miss Edmee Bowles had to flee Belgium with her mother. She couldn't know if she was a step ahead of the Nazis—or if they were a step ahead of her—but she wouldn't go without her Belco. In the U.S. Belco sired Dogs for Defense stalwarts and helped Miss Bowles found her du Clos des Cerberes kennel. At Belco's left is his son by Ch. Lisa, Ch. Marius du Clos des Cerbres. And on the right is Ch. Lisa CD.

Westergoo, the first American champion. Bojar, bred in 1935 by J. Ferwerda in Leeuwarden, The Netherlands, was imported by Young. Ch. Milton, Lisa, Mary Pickford du Pandore, Sultan and Samlo figure in his pedigree. The Bojar-Laraine mating produced three notable bitches, Asta, Inga and Caprice. The last named was presented by Bliss to the then Jacqueline Bouvier who subsequently showed her at Westminster in 1942.

In 1940 the Youngs finished a Bojar daughter, Lisa, with Miss Edmee Bowles handling her to the title. Lisa was bred to her sire, producing a large litter. Most of these puppies went on to serve in the Coast Guard's Dogs for Defense program. Again Miss Bowles was there with her great feeling for dogs and her especial knowledge of the Bouviers of her native land. She assisted Coast Guard Commander Newbolt Ely in the training of these dogs. One Coast Guard Bouvier, owned by Adam M. Butler, was killed on Salerno's beaches.

Bred to Miss Bowles' Belco, Ch. Lisa CD produced Ch. Marius du Clos des Cerberes, still fondly remembered by Miss Bowles as one of the finest she ever owned.

Beeta Van Wakershof, whelped in 1944 was sold in 1948 to Mrs. L. de Rochemont of New Hampshire. She joined an import, Czardas Van Het BunderBosch, whelped in 1938, which Mr. de Rochemont had bought from M. Widdershoven in Bunda. Czardas' classic pedigree is quickly traced to such early foundation stock as Ch. Milton, Dragon de la Lys, Lydia and Arga de la Lys.

Ch. Argus de la Thudinie, our cover dog, was whelped in 1951. Bred by Justin Chastel in Belgium he was a significant winner and

Ch. Bel Echo du Clos de Cerberes was a show winner in the 1954-55 era. Sired by Ch. Marius du Clos des Cerberes out of Ch. Ellyrdia, he was owned by Katherine Walker of Sewickley, Pa. Photo by Norton.

Recorded here is what may have been the turning point for the Bouvier in America. When Deewal Kennels' ten year old Argus de la Thudinie was selected as best in show at Worcester County Kennel Club in mid-December, 1961 by the late Mrs. E. P. Renner, it was the first time a Bouvier had ever won such an honor in the United States. Argus broke the ice of "no precedent" in the minds of many judges. Left to right: unidentified trophy presenter, Mrs. Renner, handler Erik Thomee and Mrs. Dorothy Walsh.

sire before importation to the U.S. in 1959 by Fred Walsh, New York advertising executive. Sired by Volpi de la Vallee de l'Escallion out of Ucaba, Argus made Bouvier history in the United States. A dog of commanding presence, he won a number of group placements.

Then, at $10\frac{1}{2}$ years he won the large and prestigious Worcester County show with the late Mrs. Edward B. Renner judging. It was the first time any Bouvier had won an American show.

It is extraordinary when any dog past his normal prime years can take a show. Only the very soundest dogs can successfully compete at an advanced age. No domestic dog is perfectly constructed. To move well each dog must make muscular compensations for whatever defects he has in his locomotive apparatus. If they are minor he can pretty well hide them—so long as he is young enough to have the strength and muscular tone to make the adjustments. When he gets tired, or old, the defects become visible in his gaits. To gait well enough to win a show at 10½ a dog would need nearly perfect moving gear. On that day Argus beat the finest dogs competing in the East. Unfortunately his eyesight began to fail and he was retired from competition shortly thereafter.

Mrs. Renner, of Lakeville, Conn., said: "I couldn't help but admire his magnificent soundness and showmanship." Famed all-breed show judge William Kendrick pronounced Argus one of the finest working dogs he had seen. He said: "Argus' recognition in the ring should have come to him much earlier."

People who had never before heard of Bouviers saw Argus' picture in newspapers and magazines. Advertising man Walsh saw to that. Public interest in Bouviers was on the rise. And, the ice had been broken insofar as dog shows were concerned. Argus had established a precedent which demanded that judges fully and properly consider every Bouvier exhibited under them.

Statistics detail the Bouvier's lengthy climb to popularity in the United States. For the first 25 years there were not sufficient Bouviers registered with the AKC to support a viable breeding program. Only through continuing importations was the breed able to sustain a presence in the U.S. during those years. It took 40 years before the breed could average over 20 AKC registrations per year.

The "rank by breed" column in the accompanying table can be a bit misleading. In the years since 1931 there has been nearly a 50% increase in the number of breeds recognized by the AKC. If we make a mental adjustment for this factor and then consider that total AKC registrations had a sustained period of unprecedented growth between 1946 and 1971, the Bouvier's performance compared with other breeds has been admirable. It was a period when every breed had to run just to hold its rank. The Bouvier did much better than that.

A sudden spurt in breed popularity—such as might be ignited by a popular TV series—leads to irresponsible breeding for profit by unfeeling market breeders. This kind of growth destroys the work of generations of conscientous breeders. Fortunately, the Bouvier's climb to popularity has been measured and each Bouvier generation, thanks to breeders' skills and devotion has been, in the large, better than the last.

RECORD OF BOUVIER DES FLANDRES REGISTRATIONS WITH THE AKC

YEAR	AKC Regs.	Cum. Totals	Cum. Av. AKC Regs. per Year from 1926	AKC Rank by Breed
1926 thru 1930	—	0	0	
1931	2	2	.33	81
1932 thru 1934	—	2	.22	
1935	1	3	.3	93
1936	5	8	.73	93
1937	7	15	1.25	88
1938	7	22	1.7	90
1939	2	24	1.7	96
1940	13	37	2.5	85
1941	8	45	2.8	87
1942	8	53	3.1	93
1943	2	55	3.0	96
1944	9	64	3.4	84
1945	3	67	3.35	91
1946	3	70	3.3	89
1947	—	70	3.2	—
1948	1	71	3.0	94
1949	14	85	3.5	94
1950	9	94	3.8	97
1951	27	121	4.6	92
1952	19	140	5.2	96
1953	16	156	5.6	88
1954	28	184	6.3	90
1955	39	223	7.4	88
1956	10	233	7.4	93
1957	26	259	8.0	92
1958	18	277	8.4	94
1959	44	321	9.4	85
1960	46	367	10.5	88
1961	59	426	11.9	89
1962	93	519	14.0	89
1963	85	604	16.0	89
1964	118	722	18.5	87
1965	130	852	21.3	89
1966	149	1,001	24.4	87
1967	221	1,222	29.5	82
1968	267	1,489	34.6	76
1969	330	1,819	41.3	76
1970	348	2,167	48.2	78
1971	367	2,534	55.0	82
1972	511	3,045	64.8	75
1973	585	3,630	75.6	77

As we shall see in later chapters the Bouvier' popularity and his service have extended into many facets of life in the United States and Canada. In public service Bouviers have served the blind, the military and in police K-9 Corps. In public competition they have proved themselves in the obedience rings and in show rings they have won high honors disproportionate to their numbers.

One of the greatest classics of dog fiction has a Bouvier as its hero. Ironically, it preceeded the Bouvier as we know the breed today. An English edition of *A Dog of Flanders—A Christmas Story,* appeared in England as early as 1872. It was authored by Louisa de la Ramé who used the pseudonym "Ouida." The story of the boy, Nello, and his dog, Patrasche, has had many subsequent editions in many languages. Here's a brief passage:[1]

Within sound of the little melancholy clock, almost from their birth upward, they had dwelt together, Nello and Patrasche, in the little hut on the edge of the village, with the cathedral spire of Antwerp rising in the northeast, beyond the great green plain of seeding grass and spreading corn that stretched away from them like a tideless, changeless sea. It was the hut of a very old man, of a very poor man—of old Jehan Daas, who in his time had been a soldier, and who remembered the wars that had trampled the country as oxen tread down the furrows, and who had brought from his service nothing except a wound, which had made him a cripple.

When old Jehan Daas had reached his full eighty, his daughter

1. The illustration is by "G. H. B." from an 1891 edition published in Boston by the Joseph Knight Co.

had died in the Ardennes, hard by Stavelot, and had left him in legacy her two-year-old son. The old man could ill contrive to support himself, but he took up the additional burden uncomplainingly, and it soon became welcome and precious to him. Little Nello—which was but a pet diminutive for Nicolas—throve with him, and the old man and the little child lived in the poor little hut contentedly.

It was a very humble little mid-hut indeed, but it was clean and white as a sea-shell, and stood in a small plot of garden-ground that yielded beans and herbs and pumpkins. They were very poor, terribly poor—many a day they had nothing at all to eat. They never by any chance had enough: to have had enough to eat would have been to have reached paradise at once. But the old man was very gentle and good to the boy, and the boy was a beautiful, innocent, truthful, tender natured creature; and they were happy on a crust and a few leaves of cabbage, and asked no more of earth or heaven; save indeed that Patrasche should be always with them, since without Patrasche where would they have been?

For Patrasche was their alpha and omega; their treasury and granary; their store of gold and wand of wealth; their bread-winner and minister; their only friend and comforter. Patrasche dead or gone from them, they must have laid themselves down and died likewise. Patrasche was body, brains, hands, head, and feet to both of them: Patrasche was their very life, their very soul. For Jehan Daas was old and a cripple, and Nellow was but a child; and Patrasche was their dog.

A dog of Flanders—yellow of hide, large of head and limb, with wolf-like ears that stood erect, and legs bowed and feet widened in the muscular development wrought in his breed by many generations of hard service. Patrasche came of a race which had toiled hard and cruelly from sire to son in Flanders many a century—slaves of slaves, dogs of the people, beasts of the shafts and the harness, creatures that lived straining their sinews in the gall of the cart, and died breaking their hearts on the flints of the streets.

Patrasche had been born of parents who had labored hard all their days over the sharp-set stones of the various cities and the long, shadowless, weary roads of the two Flanders and of Brabant. He had been born to no other heritage than those of pain and of toil. He had been fed on curses and baptized with blows. Why not? It was a Christian country, and Patrasche was but a dog. Before he was fully grown he had known the bitter gall of the cart and the collar. Before he had entered his thirteenth month he had become the property of a hardware-dealer, who was accustomed to wander over the land north and south, from the blue sea to the green mountains. They sold him for a small price, because he was so young.

In all probability *A Dog of Flanders* did inspire some Bouvier importations into both the United States and Canada. But we find no record of these importations prior to World War I. There are unconfirmed reports of importations circa 1920 to Michigan with stock spreading from there into Canada. However, since such imports left no continuing line they have left no imprint upon the history of the Bouvier.

Among the earlier American breeders and promoters of the Bouvier were Mr. and Mrs. George Butts of Springfield, Ill. Their imported Ch. Coquin de la Thudinie was the first Bouvier to win a working group first in an American Kennel Club show. They also imported Ch Draga de la Thudinie. Bred to Coquin she produced Chef de Truffe. Miss Bowles purchased Truffe and finished his championship in grand style by winning best of breed at Westchester in 1962.

It might be useful to pause here to point out how difficult it is —and how important it is—to win a working group placement in an AKC show. Take two, large, representative and recent shows. They had a total of 6,296 dogs entered in classes with group-eligible potentiality. Of the six AKC groups the sporting had 20.9% of the dogs, hound had 14.6%, terrier 9.4%, toy 10% and non-sporting 11.4%. The working group, with 33.76% comprised over one-third of the show honors-eligible entries. This is about average. These figures show it is more than half again as difficult to win a working group placement as one in the sporting group; 2.31 times harder than in the hound group; three times harder than in the non-sporting group; 3.4 times harder than in the toy group and 3.6 times harder than in the terrier group. Stated more simply, working groups with more than one-third of the competition have four group placements while the remaining two-thirds of the competition have 20 group placements to share. Dogs in other groups average a two-and-one-half times better shot at a group win. And, before a Bouvier can win a show he must first win the working group.

Evert Van de Pol, Miss Bowles, Miss Virginia Bull and Miss Janet Mack of New York City, as well as Dorothy and Fred Walsh of Flem-

This photo produced publicity for Bouviers during their earlier days in the U.S.. Evert Van der Pol sold a brindle male pup to a dog food promoter. He was one of a litter which produced Ch. Ciscoldo, Ch. Rialto and Ch. Ellydria. He was called Calo because that was the brand name of the dog food. He did his bit with the cart and stories were put out that he was 31 inches high, weighed 140 pounds—and ate six pounds of Calo daily. AKC records indicate Ch. Ciscoldo and Calo were the same dog. There was an ad painted on the front of the cart. Van der Pol wrote Janet Mack: "It was a misleading advertisement, so I've blotted it out."

ington, New Jersey, were all interested in the promotion and betterment of the breed and worked together to this end for some time. Their first dogs, most all of which were from The Netherlands, had the very short harsh wiry coats that is still seen in the Dutch strains today. Van de Pol imported Silta. She was then in whelp to the Dual Champion of Holland for four years in succession, Ch. Basko Aleida v.d. Zaanhoeve. From this litter she produced the first and second west coast champions, Ciskoldo and his litter sister, Rialto. Another puppy from this litter, Ellyrdria, was sold to Miss Bowles. She also became a champion. Silta won 12 points and a C.D.

Miss Bowles then moved toward French and Belgian breeding. She imported Wandru des Coudreaux from France in 1958 and Remado's Katleen from Belgium in 1960. Van de Pol imported Bonaparte van Darling-Astrid from the Netherlands and sold him to the Walshs' Deewal Kennels. Bonaparte became a champion but sired only one champion, Deewal Toronto.

In 1959 the Walshs joined the move toward Belgian-French breeding. They imported Argus de la Thudinie, Faussette l' Ideal de Charlerei and Hardy l' Ideal de Charleroi. These were followed later by Hion de la Thudinie, Kaline du Posty Arlequin and Irca de la Thudinie. Mrs. Marion Hubbard of Madrone Ledge acquired her first import through Miss Janet Mack. From Belgium's de la Thudinie kennel came Krepsie de la Thudinie and she became the third west coast champion and first one there in 15 years.

Even in those days of much milder inflation dogs sold to America were quite high except for Argus. He was purchased for $125.00. Hardy was $300.00 and Faussette l' Ideal de Charleroi was $500.00. It must be remembered that Argus, who figures into many pedigrees today, was $8\frac{1}{2}$ years old when imported. He was used often as a sire in Europe, and even after his arrival here, his campaigning and best in show, he produced several litters before his death at age eleven.

Recently Van de Pol, who had been inactive in breeding and showing for several years, imported a dog from the Netherlands named Quintus Astra V.D. Ouden Dijk; a dog that has gone best of breed and has earned points at western shows.

An early friend of the breed and the president of the Bouvier des Flandres Club of America was Evert van de Pol of San Francisco. Also instrumental in forming the early club was Miss Edmee Bowles, Mr. and Mrs. Louis de Rochemont, Julius Bliss and George Young.

Ch. Bonaparte van Darling-Astrid was an excellent example of the Dutch stock which was imported and bred from in the years immediately after World War II. Bred by H. M. Vougelers at Ostvoorner in 1953, he was imported by Evert Van der Pol and later sold to Deewal Kennels. Photo by Shafer.

An introduction to Bouviers diverted the attention of the late Janet W. Mack from her winning Poodles, Scotties, Doberman Pinschers—and partially from her Manchester Terriers. Near her Greenwich Village home Ch. Erlo de La Thudinie plays the Bouvier role as a giant.

Bliss was the first Bouvier breeder of record in the United States. Later on Mr. and Mrs. Fred Walsh and Mr. and Mrs. Butts, Mr. and Mrs. Butler and others tried to keep the club together and functioning.

Miss Janet Mack of New York City was a strong influence and a hard worker for the breed. She imported Erlo de la Thudinie who quickly became an American champion. Erlo was a producing sire and the foundation of the Bouvier branch of Miss Mack's famed Grenadier Kennels. Erlo sired many litters, but his litter whelped by Ch. Kaline du Posty Arlequin owned by Seymore Levine of Putnan Valley, New York, made the news pages of the New York Times. Kaline had 18 puppies in September 1962, of which 15 survived.

James Neylon imported Ch. Konard du Rotiane and Remado's Jasmine from Mssr. Dauwe. He bred Remado's Jasmine to Deewal import Ch. Hion de la Thudinie in 1964. The mating produced Ch. De Ney's Grosser Knabe who became number three Bouvier in the nation in 1966, when he took a group first at the big Trenton show.

Another early import was Etoile Des Coudreaux from Mme. A. Sernin de Leysat Corbier's kennel. Whelped in May 1955, Etoile, imported by Col. Duke, sired several litters. His quality puppies attracted the attention of several people who became serious fanicers. One such mating was to Trixie in 1958. She was owned by Dorothy E. Taylor. Trixie (Deewal's Max—Escaut de Belgique) whelped a large litter including Ch. Deewal Nicole and Devil of Story Book. Ch. Deewal Nicole bred to Ch. Argus de la Thudinie produced Ch. Demon Ripp.

The de Rochemonts were instrumental in getting Fred and Dorothy

Ch. Argus de la Thudinie in Belgium as a young dog. From the collection of Janet W. Mack.

Walsh interested in the breed. Ms. Virginia Bull became a very active member and breeder for a time. Her Peerkja O'River Oakes was an early champion. Mrs. Edith Sturges O'Conner worked for many years on behalf of the club and Bouviers.

A second attempt to form a strong working Bouvier Club of America faltered and the club became inactive. There were too many miles between owners. They were spread far apart, and communications were lacking. Owners were still few in number—and there was a need for a real catalyst.

THE ROLE OF THE BOUVIER CLUBS

IF it is to progress in quality and in popularity a breed, such as the Bouvier, needs a rallying point for its enthusiasts. Breeders and exhibitors need a base for cooperative efforts. These are just two of the reasons why breed clubs are formed. There are others.

Pioneering one of the rarer breeds to popularity can be a rather lonely undertaking. And, no matter his financial, mental and physical resources every breeder *needs* an opportunity to directly compare his stock against the creations of others active in his chosen breed. Without the opportunity of competition he cannot know if he is progressing or regressing. He cannot know how far he is ahead or behind.

Breed promotion and propagation cannot be a one man or one kennel undertaking for this very reason. In England before World War I one wealthy enthusiast almost succeeded in gaining ownership of *every* quality Flatcoated Retriever. The breed lost its momentum and almost became extinct. It is still struggling to recover.

Breed clubs can generate promotional literature. They can be available to answer questions from the public, to make referals to prospective puppy buyers, to formulate and establish a breed standard, to sponsor competitions within a breed, to assist in an exchange of information between breeders and owners—possibly through a breed publication—and become a social outlet for people with a common interest.

The Bouvier des Flandres was slow in gaining momentum in the United States until a permanent breed club was established.

Evert Van de Pol made a valiant effort to launch a national Bouvier club in the early fifties. At that time the AKC's policy required a club to gain a local foothold before it could expand to a national membership and influence. Van de Pol's Bouvier des Flandres Club of America was national in name only. The AKC restricted its activities to an area within 60 miles of San Francisco. It held only one AKC sanctioned event—a "Plan A" match in Petaluma, Calif. on January 13, 1952.

Active with Van de Pol in the BFCA were Miss Edmee Bowles, Mr. and Mrs. Roberts Butts, Jr. of Springfield, Ill., Mr. and Mrs. Louis de Rochemont of New York, Hollywood and New Hampshire, Mr. and Mrs. George Young of New Canaan, Conn. and a few other pioneers. Dorothy Young was secretary. Van de Pol lived in California. Most of the rest were on the east coast. Distances apparently were too great—and the time for a national Bouvier club had not come. The BFCA faltered and became inactive.

In November of 1962 Carl May, Jr. and John Elliott discussed the need for a national Bouvier club at the Back Mountain Kennel Club dog show. They felt the time for such an organization had arrived.

May and Elliott compiled a mailing list and sent invitations to an organizational meeting held in connection with the Philadelphia show in December. Seventeen people attended. A committee of Miss Edmee Bowles, John Elliott, Carl May, Jr., Mrs. Edith Sturges O'Connor and Fred Walsh was appointed to draft a constitution and by-laws—and otherwise get things started. It conducted a survey of breeders and owners so the club could cater to the real wants and needs of prospective members. Invitations were then mailed for a first annual meeting on Feb. 11, 1963 in conjunction with the Westminster show in New York. After Westminster's entry of 11 Bouviers had been judged, 21 breed enthusiasts met at the Picadilly Hotel. Fifty-four charter members were enrolled.

The organizational name selected was the American Bouvier des Flandres Club. Elected the first president was Mrs. Edith O'Connor. Miss Edmee Bowles became the initial vice-president, Joan Elliott the secretary and Carl May, Jr., the treasurer. Elected to the board of governors were Mrs. Virginia Bull, Gerald Jacoby, James Neylon and Fred Walsh. John Elliott was chairman.

The time was right. Within six months the club membership had

Carl May, Jr. with John Elliott was responsible for calling the organizational meeting of the American Bouvier des Flandres Club. He's shown here with the best of opposite sex Bouvier at the ABFC's first specialty in 1965. Selected over 44 entries was Ch. Giaconda du Clos des Cerberes.

grown to 72. In October the AKC gave tentative approval to the club's constitution. A first sanction match under "Plan B" was held the same month at Fred and Dorothy Walsh's Deewal Kennels in Flemington, N.J. There was an entry of 32. After the AKC-imposed six month interval, in April 1964 the second "Plan B" match was held. The AKC then approved a "Plan A" match which drew 43 entries in October of 1964. Right on schedule, in April 1965, the second "Plan A" match was held. The ABFC thus completed all of the prerequisites for the offering of an AKC-recognized specialty show. It was almost exactly three years from the first organizational meeting in Philadelphia to the first specialty in the same location. Exhibitors responded with 44 entries, and specialties have been held continuously since.

The Societe Royale Saint Hubert records her as Lumina, LOSH 86108, a brindle bred by J. Josis of Cuesmes, Belgium from Cleps de la Ville des Doges—Herbelotte du Prefeuillet and whelped March 26, 1937. The AKC records her as Lumina, A270003, owned by Virginia de Rochemont. To the de Rochemonts she was Rita who warned them immediately whenever their young Louis showed symptoms of insulin shock. She so infused the de Rochemonts with appreciation for Bouviers they continue as owners and breeders 37 years later. Also in appreciation they commissioned Holden D. Wetherbee to execute this etching of Rita, of which only six prints were pulled.

The American Bouvier des Flandres Club became a member club of the American Kennel Club in 1971. Today the club has a membership of over 140 and continuing healthy growth. The ABFC's secretary's name and address are listed in each issue of the AKC's official publication, *Pure-Bred Dogs,* under "Member Clubs." The monthly is available in many libraries. Another means of obtaining the ABFC's address is by request to the American Kennel Club at 51 Madison Avenue, New York, N.Y. 10010.

THE BELGIAN CHALLENGE AND THE DOROTHY WALSH TROPHIES

TWO trophies represent achievement of the ultimate—or nearly so—for exhibitors at the American Bouvier des Flandres Club's annual specialty shows.

Although it is very young in comparison with other AKC "parent" clubs the American Bouvier des Flandres Club is already establishing tradition in its competitions. The AKC no longer approves the introduction of perpetual trophies but challenge trophies, as attainable objectives, heighten the zest and the quality of competition. The Dorothy Walsh Challenge Trophy is an extension of Mrs. Walsh's dedication to constant improvement of quality in Bouviers. The beautiful 14-inch silver-plated punch bowl first went into competition at the annual Bouvier specialty in Philadelphia on Dec. 11, 1971.

For permanent possession the Walsh trophy must be won three times by the same owner, not necessarily with the same dog. A smaller silver-plated trophy is awarded outright to commemorate each qualifying win.

The Walsh trophy is awarded to the owner of the best of winners. When it was placed in competition it was thought the bowl would be quite safe from early retirement. Here's why. Any Bouvier good enough to win a leg on it would almost certainly win its championship during the year intervening before the next specialty. (Although

The first Bouvier to win a leg on the Dorothy Walsh Challenge Trophy (in front of placement sign) was barely old enough to compete in an AKC show. In 1971 Duxbury House's Ulrich was carried by Judge Joseph Mellor all of the way from the junior puppy dog class through winners dog to best of winners at the American Bouvier des Flandres Club's annual specialty show. It was a five point major, putting the youngster one-third of the way toward a championship. The next year his kennel mate, Bras de Fer Terry, was best of winners—thus gaining a second leg for the Bras de Fer Kennel of Mr. and Mrs. Frank Mees of West Chester, Pa. Photo by Gilbert.

eligible for the open class champions are almost never entered there. Exhibitors almost universally choose to avoid insofar as possible situations where their champions might be beaten by non-champions.) For Bouviers it is the year's toughest class competition. The chances of any one owner coming up with three dogs good enough—and just far enough along in their bench campaigning to be class-eligible at the specialty—is quite remote. But, events do not always respect the odds. One owner won legs during each of the first two years the Walsh trophy was in competition. For Mr. and Mrs. Frank Mees of West Chester, Pa. and their Bras de Fer Kennels, Duxbury House's Ulrich was b-w in 1971 and Terry Bras de Fer, a bitch, was b-w in 1972.

The Belgian Challenge Trophy is even more prestiguous—and much more difficult of attainment. It was donated by the Club National Belge du Bouvier des Flandres under conditions so severe it can neither be described in the show catalog nor be presented at or during the show. It does not have official AKC status—but it certainly does have enormous status with Bouvier owners.

The Belgian Trophy, a hand-wrought, chased, pewter tray of approximately 24 inches diameter, is awarded to the annual specialty's best of breed if that winner was bred in the United States by the owner at the time of showing. A smaller replica goes with each leg won. Outright possession requires three consecutive wins—or five wins over a period of more than three years. With all imported, purchased, inherited, or gift dogs ineligible, it can be seen that before the Belgian Challenge is eventually retired there will be many years when no leg is awarded. It was intended to be a longterm motivator for Americans to breed and show their own quality Bouviers. It should continue to be just that for a very long time.

EUROPEAN KENNELS

THE European kennels which are of the greatest interest to Americans and Canadians are those which developed and bred from the foundation dogs, and those that have exported worthwhile breeding and show stock to North America. In most instances those who guarded and refined the breed were also prominent among those who sold good dogs to America. Many of the names encountered in the chapter on Bouvier history will be recorded again in this chapter dealing with important and helpful exporters.

Many extended pedigrees of today's winning dogs show the names of Yoja and Ucaba and others carrying the suffix of Victor Martinage, "de la Ville des Doges."

It would be impossible to overly honor the contributions of the late Florimond E. Verbanck of Ghent who used the suffix, "de Royghem." His diplomacy in keeping French and Belgian breeders working together was only one of his contributions. Like Victor Martinage, he was a highly respected international judge and a dedicated breeder, exhibitor, guardian and promoter of Bouviers.

M. Verbanck had an excellent command of the English language and he gave wise counsel to several generations of North American Bouvier fanciers. A faithful correspondent, his help was always available for the asking. And, he was a gracious host to the many Americans who made the pilgrimage to his kennel. He was in his 83rd year in 1971 when he retired from breeding and shows.

The late Florimond E. Verbanck of Ghent was friend and counselor to virtually all Bouvier breeders in Belgium and the United States during recent years. An early American Bouvier des Flandres Club specialty's best of breed trophy was dedicated in his honor. He was secretary of the Club National Belge du Bouvier des Flandres until well into his 83rd year. It was M. Verbanck who responded to most queries from overseas. He translated for other breeders who did not have a command of English and he infused many with his enthusiasm for and dedication to Bouviers.

Verbanck paid a towering tribute to Justin Chastel of Thuin, Belgium. He said Chastel had "created the modern Bouvier"—that Chastel had bred a distinctive line of such quality that it had, little by little, become the standard of "type" for the breed.

Justin Chastel began his show career in 1932—as a losing exhibitor. His successes began after he purchased, in 1936, a three-year-old bitch named Albionne de Biercee. Her sire, Follie du Ci Blanc, was widely considered the best male of his time. Follie had lost an ear in a fight so Chastel was able to buy him, also.

Then, exhibiting the kind of objectivity which distinguishes outstanding breeders, Chastel passed over his own celebrated stud to use a male he considered a superior mate for Albionne. From her litter by Klaas du Pandore he kept one male, Lucifer de la Thudinie—and thereby launched a great kennel.

Bred back to his dam, Lucifer produced Mirette de la Thudinie. She was soon established as one of Belgium's top ranked Bouviers. Then the Nazis overran Belgium. Mirette was sent to stay with a

Justin Chastel and his son with, respectively, the winning team and the winning brace at a Brussels show about 1957. De la Thudinie has been deep in quality Bouviers for nearly three decades.

Justin Chastel of de la Thudinie, left, with his friend and mentor, the late Florimond E. Verbanck.

farmer friend in the hope that the blight of war would spare both people and dogs and better days would come. Breeding was beyond contemplation. No one could know how long the war might last. Finally, in 1944, Chastel brought Mirette home.

Chastel knew what he liked and he had the courage of his convictions. He selected for Mirette a stud he fancied but which had never been shown. Adolphe Meeus' Joris de Ble d'Or and Mirette produced Soprano de la Thudinie. At the first post-war show in Binche Soprano was something of a sensation. He won the CAC in males and his dam did the same in the classes for females. Soprano went on to an international title and highly rewarding victories. From that point on de la Thudinie dogs have won consistently for M. Chastel and they've won wherever Bouviers have been shown.

Poisoning, the details of which were not disclosed, killed twelve young dogs of the Chastel kennel in 1969. This slowed Chastel's show exhibiting until 1971—but it didn't stop him. His Quarine de la Thudinie won a RCACIB at Paris in 1970. In March of 1972 his Tina de la Thudinie won the CACIB in Paris. At the same show Uhlan de la Thudinie was rated the top young male and Tina received the same award in the young female class. Tina won another CACIB soon after in Luxemburg and went on to defeat the only Bouvier rated ahead of her in Paris.

M. Chastel has assumed at least a part of Florimond Verbanck's role as advisor to those who feel a need to write to "headquarters" for information about Bouviers. However he is not conversant in English as M. Verbanck was.

Edward Moreaux of Brussels, now deceased, made his I'Ile Monsin kennel name famous worldwide. His breeding won at European shows over a period of many years. A recent AKC champion from his kennel is Poukydel I'Ile Monsin. Whelped in 1966, Poukydel was imported and is owned by Isaiah V. Oglesby of Michigan.

Because he came upon the scene some years after Chastel, Felix Grulois, also of Thuin, had the opportunity to build upon Chastel's success. His "du Posty Arlequin" suffix has become as famed in North America as it is in Europe.

Grulois' first exports to the United States came in the early 60's and proved significant more as producers than as show campaigners. Ch. Kaline du Posty Arlequin was prolific; in one litter she whelped 18 living Bouviers—and raised 15 of them. Ch. Nota du Posty Arlequin was an excellent producing dam for Robert Abady.

Int. Ch. Soprano de la Thudinie (Joris du Ble d'Or— Mirette de la Thudinie) was the post-war foundation sire for Justin Chastel. He was a sensation on the bench—even greater as a producer. Saga de la Thudinie, center, by Rico de la Thudinie out of Quattiona de la Thudinie, was whelped in 1969, the year Chastel lost a number of dogs in a poisoning incident. She is owned by Serge Shire. Usar de la Thudinie's coat was still wet when he was photographed (right) immediately after competing in a working trial. In 1968 he was champion of France.

One of Grulois' first Bouviers was Idole du Posty Arlequin. From Ch. Job de la Thudinie she produced for him Linouche du Posty Arlequin—dam of several outstanding winners, some of which were sold to the United States. Eliane de la Thudinie was also purchased from Chastel. Like Idole she was bred to Job and this mating did much to establish the du Posty Arlequin line. In the litter was Liska du Posty Arlequin that became the dam of one of the top bitches in American Bouvier history, Ch. Odelette du Posty Arlequin. Eliane also produced the dam of Johane du Posty Arlequin when bred to Bonzo l'Ideal de Charleroi. And, Johane is the mother of the all-time show-winning Bouvier, Chester Collier's Naris du Posty Arlequin.

Naris was sired by one of the greatest champions of the continent, Ch. Marc de la Thudinie.

As might be presumed, neighbors Chastel and Grulois have worked together for many years and the latter credits Chastel with important guidance and instruction. To some extent they still intermingle breeding lines.

Grulois, his wife and their three children do not have an enormous kennel from which to operate. But, because the kennel is in their backyard they have every opportunity to study closely each of their 20 or so adult Bouviers. (Not all are breeding stock. Some are canine pensioners.) So it is really from a quite modest base that Grulois has achieved so much.

Naris has now retired to grace and guard the Collier's Irvington-on-Hudson home, but his success as a campaigner created a heavy demand for du Posty Arlequin Bouviers. Grulois resisted any temptation to inflate his breeding program and thereby capitalize on the situation. Some of the dogs he sold to America since have made fine show records. One is Ch. Picolette du Posty Arlequin, the top-winning Bouvier bitch in AKC show history. Another is Ch. Raby du Posty Arlequin. Two that have been fruitful producers of quality are Ch. Sadine du Posty Arlequin imported and owned by Dr. and Mrs. Arthur Pedersen and Tania du Posty Arlequin, owned and appreciated by Miss Bowles.

The late Auguste Framshet bred some of the earlier notables. His Ike de Belgique and Fricko de Belgique are sires prominent in many modern pedigrees.

Charleroi, near the French border, is a city with a great dog show. Interest in pure-breds runs high there and Lebon used the name for

Calli des Coudreaux was bred by Madam Sornin de Leysat of Mantfermeil, France. He won the CACIB in Paris in 1956.

Whelped in June 1970 Tania du Posty Arlequin (Rico de la Thudinie—Praline du Posty Arlequin) was imported by Miss Edmee Bowles in 1972, shortly after this photo was taken.

Four excellent fronts are evident in this unposed photo of Demoiselle, Eliane, Irca and Hulotte de la Thudinie. Demoiselle was the dam of Ch. Hion de la Thudinie. Eliane became an important foundation dam in the breeding program of Felix Grulois' du Posty Arlequin kennel. Irca later became an AKC champion.

his "l'Ideal de Charleroi" kennel of winning Bouviers. Bonzo l'Ideal de Charleroi is in the pedigrees of many outstanding dogs. He sired Ch. Konrad du Rotiane. Konrad's dam was Hosca l'Ideal de Charleroi, a great bitch of her time.

The name, "du Ble d'Or" was established by Adolphe Meeus of Belgium. His most notable stud was Joris du Ble d'Or that sired International Ch. Soprano de la Thudinie. Soprano was an outstanding producer. He sired Ucaba, Victor Martinage's dog. When bred to his daughter he produced Zolla de la Thudinie, dam of the first important American sire, Ch. Coquin de la Thudinie. Coquin, in turn, sired Ch. Chief de Truffe.

The "des Coudreaux" prefix belongs to Madam Sornin de Leysat of Montfermeil, France. She has campaigned her Bouviers successfully over most of Europe. Their progeny are prominent in many American pedigrees.

Ch. Wandru des Coudreaux was another of Miss Bowles' imports. She was a litter sister to Wanda des Coudreaux—and Wanda was the dam of the 1953 champion of the year at the Paris International show, Ch. Ygor des Coudreaux. Among Ygor's get, the most important to American breeders was the aforementioned Coquin de la Thudinie imported by Mr. and Mrs. George Butts of Springfield, Ill. Coquin was the first Bouvier to win an AKC working group.

Joan Butts was among the first of the American breeders to travel to Europe in search of Bouvier breeding stock. Some notes she made in the '50s reflect the inclination of American breeders of that period to look to Dutch breeders. However, this was about the time she imported Coquin and Draga de la Thudinie from Justin Chastel, the first breeder on her list.

Of Florimond Verbanck she wrote: "He is secretary of the Belgian Bouvier Club. When I wrote several Belgian breeders he replied for them because none spoke English. He does." Her notes continued, "Mr. and Mrs. Vacheniius de Jongh, Hasseltsestraat 27, Scheveningen, Holland. He is a retired ship captain and speaks English. She does not. She runs obedience classes in and around Scheveningen, a suburb of The Hague.

"Dr. Vervoorn-Malinosky Blom, Roelofsstraat 54, The Hague, Holland. She is a veterinarian, speaks fluent English. Our last puppy from her.

"S. v.d. Waardt, Buurtweg 88a, Wassenaar, Holland. I believe he is

Kaline, Irca, Job and Ketty de la Thudinie comprise a formidable quartet of Bouviers.

Quelly, Pia and Quiar de la Thudinie were whelped in 1966 (Pia) and 1967 as indicated by their names. Quiar was exported to Deewal kennels. Irca de la Thudinie, bottom left, a producing dam, was whelped in June 25, 1959. Ch. Job de la Thudinie, bottom right, was an important sire for both the de la Thudinie and the du Posty Arlequin kennels. Job and Irca's photos by Dethuin.

Victor Martinage's Yoja (LOSH 152360) is one of the few Bouviers ever to win an international show in Europe. She did it in March 1952. She was by Tory de Groeninghe, he by Simba de la Ville des Dosges (sic) out of Ria van de Mandelstad. Her dam was Trika de Groeninghe, she by Roby-Dy de la Ville des Doges out of Sarah van't Kantientje. Thus Yoja's grandsires were both of Martinage's own breeding. Here Martinage wins the "grand prize" with her in Utrecht, The Netherlands. Photo by Jolas, Graverbage.

Imported by Deewal kennels Ch. Hion de la Thudinie reigned three years ('62–'64) as the top show-winning Bouvier in the U.S. His sire was the Moreaux-bred Cendrillo de l'Ile Monsin and his dam Demoiselle de la Thudinie. His winning get included Ch. Job de la Thudinie.

"Rouge Pommier" at the 1971 Bouvier specialty show on the Paris estate of Gilbert Thorp in June 1971 was Ringo de la Thudinie. A study of this photo can demonstrate better than any words the desired cobbiness in Bouviers.

Justin Chastel has called Marc de la Thudinie, whelped in 1963, the greatest dog he has ever owned. Marc was best in show at Brussels and at Charleroi. Importer Robert Abady has been no less enthusiastic. Marc has headed Abady's des Preux Vuilbaard kennel and proven himself an outstanding sire.

Florimond Verbanck called Ygor des Coudreaux, left, and Almyre des Coudreaux "a magnificent brace of Bouviers." Both were bred by Mme. Sorin de Leysat, then of Corbier, France. Ygor was whelped August 30, 1950 and Almyre less than six months later. Both were owned by Rene Canay of Seine, France. Photo by Dim.

Photos don't always do justice to their subjects. But when nothing better than this home snapshot is available of three outstanding Bouvier bitches room must be made for it. European Ch. U'Ada Gratte Salle, left, is shown with two of her daughters, Wanda des Coudreaux, center, also a champion in Europe, and Wandree a'Jioete.

So excellent did Miss Edmee Bowles consider the head and expression of Almyre des Coudreaux that she chose it as her model when drawing the official emblem of the American Bouvier des Flandres Club.

Ygor des Coudreaux was widely shown and a winner in Avignon, Tulouse, Brussels, Amsterdam, Monaco, Geneva, and Paris.
Both photos by Dim.

Ch. U'Ada du Gratte Saule was a very successful post-war campaigner. She won 12 presentations in 1948 and a total of 12 CAC's and 2 CACIB's.

a police or customs officer. He lives in the remodeled stables of a huge estate. Derby from him. One of the best looking litters of Bouviers I have ever seen. He speaks no English but knows Mr. de Jongh who can reply for him. Wassenaar is also a suburb of the Hague.

"Mrs. W. Neyenhuisen, Kromstraat 62, Oss, Holland. I have not met her and really know nothing about her or her Bouviers.

"Dr. Bernard Bourinet, Rue Lacapelle 68, Montauban (Tarn-et-Garonne), France. This veterinarian has the du Maine-Giraud line. He speaks only French but has a friend who can write in English.

"Mme. Sornin de Leysat, Avenue Vancanson 19, Montfermeil, S. et O., France. I doubt that she has an understanding of English. At least my several letters have been unanswered."

In Europe the title "champion" means considerably more than it does in the United States and Canada. Competitions there are held under the Federation Cynologique Internationale which is based in Brussels. Titles are not structured on the number of dogs defeated but on judicial evaluations of quality. Progression toward a championship can be made only at pre-designated shows. Show-qualified dogs of functional breeds—including Bouviers—must also win a working certificate before they are designated "champion."

This procedure places a strict limitation on the number of champions that can be made in any breed during a given year. So difficult is show championship qualification that exhibitors seek the working certificate qualifications as preludes to serious bench campaigning, there being little point in pursuing a championship unless a dog can go all of the way. At the designated national shows all of the best dogs are usually in competition, including entries from several neighboring countries seeking qualification for the even more difficult title of "international champion."

Even the championship *qualifying* designations are highly respected because they are difficult to achieve and because they are not awarded unless the judge feels he has found deserving quality. Puppies can change as they mature so they are ineligible for all official designations of quality. If an adult entry is the best of its sex and breed and if of approvable quality it can be awarded a C.A.C. which translates as a "certificate of aptitude to championship."

Even more coveted and thoroughly indicative of quality is the title, C.A.C.I.B. (certificate of aptitude to international beauty championship). It is available only at first class shows—in France, for example, at the Paris International.

Because of these high standards only a few Bouviers have achieved national or international championships under the FCI.

Some of the breed's early champions such as Ch. Nic de Sottegem, Chastel's Int. Ch. Soprano de la Thudinie, Ch. Konrad du Rotiane, and Madame Leysat's Ch. Ygor des Coudreaux have already been mentioned. So have Ch. Milton, Ch. Draga Coralie de Sottegem and Ch. Dragon de la Lys. Other early giants included Ch. Francoeur de Liege and Verbanck's Ch. Volpi de la Vallee l 'Ecaillon.

Later Belgian Bouvier champions include Chastel's Ch. Riva de la Thudinie, Ch. Job de la Thudinie (1963), Ch. Marc de la Thudinie, and Ch. Olaf de la Thudinie (1965). His Ch. Ninette de la Thudinie was exported to Carl May, Jr. and John Elliott. She was the last Belgian champion Bouvier to come to America. Ninette had won best in show at Brussels.

IMPORTING A BOUVIER

NORTH American Bouvier breeders have been extremely dependent in the past upon imported dogs to improve and replenish their breeding stock. The greatest winners have been, almost exclusively, imported dogs. Now western hemisphere breeders may be at a turning point.

Bouvier popularity on this side of the Atlantic has had a very healthy growth. There are sufficient quality Bouviers here that universal objectivity and close cooperation between our breeders could project homebred Bouvier quality the equal of any. There are already some indications that such a shift is underway.

But, there is no need for any countries without quarantines to be insular in their breeding programs. Jet flights make the shipment of dogs across boundaries and oceans quick, relatively inexpensive, accessible to virtually all and, theoretically at least, safe and humane.

We can, in fact, look ahead to enjoying the fruits of research by Dr. Stephen W. J. Seager at the University of Oregon sponsored by the AKC, and the work of other scientists. Dr. Seager is already, by using improved and carefully controlled laboratory techniques, achieving a pregnancy rate equal to natural from matings via frozen and stored semen. Semen banks and such other techniques as egg removal, storage and implantation, ovarian transplants and in-laboratory fertilization promise future breeders tools whose potentialities dazzle the imagination. For example: Dr. Seager is looking ahead to the day when eggs might be extracted from a prize bitch in the United States, then frozen and stored. Semen from a Belgian stud could be similarly frozen and stored. Sufficient semen and eggs could then be flown to, say, Australia. (By storing the material for the required quarantine period while the donors are closely observed it could be established that neither was a carrier of rabies or other communicable disease—so fulfilling the purposes of Australia's quarantine.) In the country where stored semen and stored eggs meet they could be thawed. The eggs could then be fertilized in a laboratory and then placed in the body of a healthy host mother. Thus a puppy could be whelped in Australia from a dam in North America and a sire in Europe.

This and other projections of today's researches will virtually eliminate time and international boundaries as handicaps to breeders. But, they are slightly into the future as anything more than laboratory experiments. They *do* inform us of the direction of future breedings. They *do* tell us dog breeding will be conducted on an international scale and they portend international registrations (with more uniform concepts and requirements) and international competitions (with more uniform concepts and rules). Breeders who prefer to be rather ahead than behind the times might be well advised to be thinking internationally *now*.

In former times selections for importation into America were made by agents for the purchaser—either a resident of the exporting country or an American professional who traveled abroad on buying trips. A few men made careers in such trade.

Now jet travel, inexpensive in time and money, has put Europe within the reach of all who can afford to realistically contemplate dog importation.

Americans and Canadians are now traveling to Europe by the millions. Most exhibitors and breeders have made at least one trip. Many of these trips have included pilgrimages to the more famous of Europe's kennels. And, the temptations to bring a dog or two home have made importers of thousands.

The author is a part of this trend. In 1973 she, with her husband, traveled to the homeland of the Bouvier to see, to visit, to research—and in hopes of finding a bitch to improve her breeding program.

There is magic in the word "dog." Between people of good will it can be an international "open sesame" to cordial hospitality and new

The author visited the Brussels home of the late Edward Moreaux's widow, he of L'Ile Monsin fame. Above right she photographed Justin and Mme. Chastel with Uberty de la Thudinie. At the Van den Rekels kennel in Holland, left, she found a warm welcome and more good Bouviers. Below, one of the last known photographs of the late Florimond Verbanck, at author's left, with Justin and Mme. Chastel in their home.

De La Thudinie Bouviers share a common exercise run and must therefore be compatable. Puppies, closed kennel on left, have their own run. Quiar de la Thudinie was posed for the portrait at center with breeder, Justin Chastel, when the future AKC champ was just maturing. At bottom is a view of another portion of the Chastel kennel and another exercise area just inside the kennel entrance. The dogs observe visitors closely but they are too well-manered to compete in raising a fuss.

Mrs. Robert Butts, Jr., pioneer importer, breeder and exhibitor of Bouviers in the U.S. with two imports that helped to establish the breed in America. On the left is Ch. Coquin de la Thudinie, and Ch. Draga de la Thudinie. Coquin was the second Bouvier to win an AKC championship. From the collection of the late Janet W. Mack.

friendships. Among appreciators of Bouviers there is an instant opportunity for rapport. Such was our experience.

Our search for Bouviers and Bouvier history began in Brussels. After some difficulty we located the widow of Edward Moreaux, he of L'Ile Monsin fame. The gracious lady proudly showed us photos, ribbons and other mementos of the kennel's great dogs and their triumphs. The dogs had gone to Justin Chastel's de la Thudinie kennel in Thuin—and that was our next stop.

At Chastel's lovely villa we saw quality Bouviers in abundance. Our first impression was of cleanliness and neatness in and about the kennel. Then we were nearly transfixed by the personalities and the quality of five bitches he showed us. His most prized bitch, Tina de la Thudinie, was not for sale at any price. His Belgian Ch. Riva de la Thudinie was equally treasured. We were taken with a bitch he was then breeding to a young male he esteemed very highly, Tapin de la Thudinie. Silette de la Thudinie's personality, her Bouvier character and her sweet nature captivated us. We could not believe Silette was attack trained until M. Chastel demonstrated her prowess to us. In conformation and bloodlines she offered much that we wanted to add to our breeding program. After brief negotiation she was ours.

Whist des Bois des Saules was, possibly, Europe's winningest fawn in the early '50s. He totaled three CACIBs, 19 CACs and 13 RCACs.

Tina de la Thudinie is the current pride of Justin Chastel's kennel. He has refused to put a price on her and has, in fact, declined some very generous offers.

Happiness for an American Bouvier buff is attending the Bouvier specialty match on the estate of Gilbert Thorp near Paris, especially if it is a beautiful, sweater-weather day—just right for dogs and people.

While in Thuin we were not about to miss the opportunity to meet Felix Grulois and see his du Posty Arlequin kennel. The Grulois were gracious and the Bouviers were abundant. The establishment is smaller but of equal quality to that of M. Chastel. Puppies were peeking at us from around corners and displaying all of their winning ways. We were especially impressed with a young bitch, Ultima de la Thudinie that has since taken several prizes at Belgian shows.

In the Flemish countryside we visited the De Brochian kennel where we thought the Bouviers very good in temperament and type. There the top winning campaigner and brood bitch is Querida de la Thudinie that has been rated "excellent" at shows. Her daughter, Undine de Bronchain, is a young adult full of promise.

Mr. and Mrs. de Blanders have been breeding Bouviers for many years under the tuteledge of Justin Chastel. Their "Ten Roobos" suffix is encountered in the pedigrees of many quality Bouviers of today. For examples: Milord Ten Roobos and Quitus Ten Roobos.

A delightful day was spent with Miss Julia Von Vorst at her Ouden Dyk kennel. A Bouvier breeder for over 40 years, she has exported many fine dogs to North America. She exported Ch. Boris von Ouden Dyk to the Millers in Michigan, one of the earlier quality Bouviers in that area. Evert van de Pol, inactive in Bouviers for several years, has had a resurgence of interest and is showing his imported Qunitus von Owden Dyk.

While in the Netherlands we took the opportunity to visit the Van de Rekels kennel of Miss Vermuellen in Soest.

Miss Vermullen showed us a big three year old male, Breston Xandra v.d. Rakkers. Sired by Arnaud Wally v.d. Rekels he was out of Xandra Peggy v.d. Rakkers. Their pedigrees are exclusively Dutch. They show no infusions, at least not recently, of Belgian bloodlines.

The Dutch customarily use the name of the dam in a registered name. Exandra Peggy v.d. Rakkers' name indicates she is out of a Peggy, in this instance Peggy Herta v.d. Rakkers.

The Belgian and French breeders give all puppies whelped in a given year names beginning with the letter of the alphabet designated for that year. These follow in alphabetical sequence. Dogs with "U" names were whelped in 1971. In 1972 names such as Vlada, Vertu, Vonike and Victor were used. Some American breeders have chosen to follow this rather sensible custom.

We journeyed through the countryside of Holland and Belgium, down through Normandy and into Paris. There we attended a Bouvier specialty match held at the magnificent villa of M. Gilbert Thorp.

Many Bouviers were assembled on the green, sunlit lawns of the rolling grounds—all parading at the ends of leashes held by proud owners. Here we saw the bloodlines of de la Thudinie and du Posty Arlequin in abundance. Mr. and Mr. Gelineau of Le Blanc have established the Du Clos Des Jeunes Plantes suffix. They are generally considered the most successful Bouvier breeders in France. Their stud, Quarl du clos des Jeunes Plantes Karl de L'Ile Monsin-Ninon des Casseaux) won the best male and best Bouvier awards. The top rated female Bouvier was Twiggy du Posty Arlequin owned by a Miss Nicolle, also of Le Blanc. Victor Martinage judged the males and D. Le Lann judged the females. Between them and with the assistance of Mr. Thorp they chose the best in match.

With our our homeward trip approaching we felt excited and anxious to get our new Bouviers home. Justin Chastel made all arrangements for necessary[1] papers, health certificates, vaccines and pedigree forms. We notified the airline we would be traveling with one mature Bouvier bitch and two puppies.

The airline sold us two big dog crates. From our seats we watched the dogs being loaded into the hold.

In August Silette de la Thudinie whelped and raised eight puppies. They are registered as being imported "in uttero" with Justin Chastel properly listed as their breeder. We kept Deewal Victor and Deewal Victoria. The Hubbards of Madrone Ledge took Deewal Vlinda. The James Seghers of California purchased Deewal Vonika de la Thudinie. Miss Anne Ebert, also of California took another of Silette's hopefuls. Deewal Volt went to Miss Teresa Troy and another pup was

---

1. There should also be a bill of sale or equivalent showing the sale price of the dog. The U.S. still has a ridiculous import duty on dogs not intended for breeding purposes. Since this is just about the only possible reason for importing a dog of value, the duty is only rarely collected with justification. Except that it is almost always collected at the point of entry—and then refunded when the proper papers are filed in proper form in proper sequence and on schedule. Customs should be notified of intention to file for a refund and the proper forms secured and executed *at the time of entry*. The Treasury Department has told the House Ways and Means Committee this levy costs the Treasury more to handle than it produces in revenue. The Agriculture Department has informed the same group that the duty is a pointless expense to administer. However, the law remains on the books. (Ed.)

flown to William Marshall in Denver. The eighth pup went to Alger Ashley of Michigan.

Breeders of record for Silette's brood we may not be—but we are *acting* like breeders. We're encouraging the new owners to show. We say we want the pups to have their chances—and that is true. But, it is also true that we want to find out what the pups can do.

BELCO AND I

by Miss Edmee F. Bowles

> *The story of the Bouvier in America is characterized by the story of Miss Edmee Bowles and her Belco. Both were natives of Flanders. Both served in the struggle against the Nazis, first in Belgium, then in France, and finally in the United States. Together they took up a new life here and stayed to demonstrate to all who would look or listen the joys and advantages of a Bouvier's companionship. Their arrival was the beginning of Bouvier popularity in the United States. Miss Bowles has been an active and successful breeder, trainer and exhibitor during all of the years since. She has worked selflessly with dedication, ability and enthusiasm.*
>
> *During the last three-plus decades Miss Bowles has been advisor, translator, worker in breed promotional campaigns, club member and official. Virtually every American Bouvier breeder has known her as a source of excellent stock, as a friend and as a delightful companion.*
>
> *The terrors of World War II are matters Miss Bowles has pushed to the back of her mind. She prefers happier memories but her story is so much the story of the Bouvier's emigration to America that she was persuaded to tell it here in her own words. Editor.*

Belco is credited by Miss Edmee Bowles with several times saving the lives of her mother and herself during their escape from the Nazis across Belgium and France and into Spain and Portugal. When Miss Bowles and Belco arrived in the United States in May, 1942 they became the forerunners of—and important factors in—the Bouvier's popularity growth in America. Whelped in November, 1935, Belco died in 1947. This photo was taken in 1942.

I was born in Antwerp, Belgium. My mother was Belgian and my father English and Scotch. World War I drove us from our home to England. After the armistice I stayed to complete my art studies. I was also interested in breeding and feeding experiments.

In 1932 I returned to Belgium, rejoining my mother who had bought a property in Schilde, about ten miles east of Antwerp on the main road to the German border. The area is known as Campine. It is a flat land with many pine woods.

The old farmhouse had been blown up during world War I. A new villa, Norman style, had been built on an elevation. It was of solid brick with huge chimneys. The house had two secret hiding places. Its builders had remembered the first World War when the Germans took all the valuables—silver, copper and even woolen blankets.

We had about five acres in the front of the house which we laid out with a vegetable garden and fruit trees. A long driveway, about 200 yards, led to the highway where the Belgian army had built a new blockhouse. The drive was bordered with an old copper beech hedge on one side and a wide border of flowers that bloomed from early spring until late fall on the other. Many a motorist would stop to admire the vista with the large meadows, dotted here and there with our prize goats and Westphalian geese.

We had a splendid view from our veranda. A large bell hung on the wall. Beyond were the wide rustic gates, the garage, buildings for stock, stables, a barn and the tenant farmer's house. Then there were more meadows and pine woods. Here our dogs ran freely to guard the property. There had been many robberies and trouble with poachers. Several gamekeepers had been injured and their dogs killed. Next to us was about 2,000 acres belonging to the Baroness of Schilde.

The Dutch Sheepdog we acquired with the house had been beaten almost to death. At first I had some Belgian Sheepdogs, German Shepherds and a couple of Bouvier des Flandres puppies, Dash, a female and Dombey, a male. There was also a terrier that was never home when he was needed.

My Bouviers grew into large, rustic dogs with rough coats, beards, mustaches and whiskers. I was impressed by the way these dogs of Flanders stayed home and by their effectiveness in herding cattle, even when working alone. Little by little the Bouviers superseded all the other breeds. They took over all the chores. The Bouvier is tough when necessary but he isn't mean or trecherous. His presence is a deterrent to wrongdoers. He commands respect with his dignified and determined demeanor.

In the village we formed a club, "Watch and Guard." I was manager. Various breeds came for training. First there were the usual obedience lessons: heel, forward, right and left by word or gesture. Then: jump, scale walls, find the man or object, defend, disarm, bring the man back and, of course, announce. Each dog had to be staunch to gunfire. I took my young Bouviers along and let them watch the older dogs working. They took to the training naturally.

When I acquired Belco he was just ten months old. No one foresaw his illustrious future. He had just recovered from distemper. He was a stoic, an observor and bystander. Other club members made fun saying: "That dog! He would not even say 'boo' to a goose." Dash had won the silver medal as the best working and attack dog. She saw to Belco's training.

Belco learned about the responsibilities of being a Bouvier one day

Miss Bowles has always been aware of the advantages of dramatizing the capabilities and the nature of Bouviers. She has put on many demonstrations at dog shows and other events. She obtained a Belgian dog cart and used it in publicity efforts and charity drives. Here three of her early favorites, Ch. Ellydria, Ch. Marius du Clos des Cerberes and Elfrieda du Clos des Cerberes are seen in a three-dog hitch.

when I drove to a nearby village. While in a shop I left my little niece in the car and the care of Dash and Belco. I was told later what happened. Some young hoodlums tried to get in the car. Dash knew *she* could handle the situation, but it seemed she thought Belco should face up to the situation. Belco wasn't making a move so she pushed, tugged and nipped until the light hit him. He lurched at the hoodlums with a roar!

As the hoodlums ran off Dash sat back. Her body language seemed to say: "At last it has penetrated his thick skull." From then on Belco recognized his duties and took them seriously. Interestingly, he was thereafter the unquestioned leader but he always deferred to Dash.

One morning we found one of my prize turkeys dead on the roost showing little sign of violent struggle. There was only a small puncture in the skull. Our tenant farmer suggested a weasel. That night, shod in high riding boots and armed with a club and flashlight I, with my faithful followers, laid in wait for the killer. Making my rounds I saw a huge, solitary rat. He was standing on his hind legs, hissing and prefering a fight to flight. He defied the dogs. They hesitated and I gave the command: "Attack!" The rat curled himself around one dog's muzzle. It was over like lightning. Before the rat could bite the other dogs destroyed him. He was about the length of a Dachshund. Rats are cunning. I once saw one on his back cuddling an egg while another rat was dragging him by the tail.

The summer of 1939 brought portents and the fear of war. Hitler's defiance and his tank-rattling tested the will of Europe's other powers. They let him retake the Saar which Germany had lost to France in a League of Nations plebiscite. German troops occupied the Sudetenland and annexed Austria. At Munich there was another yielding. Then—the invasion of Poland and the war was on.

France was foolishly dependent upon what it thought was the impregnable Maginot Line of fortifications. It mobilized but there was decay within its government.

In Belgium, also, there was general mobilization. Hitler had said he would never invade Belgium. Some, even in our army, believed him—probably more out of hope than logic. Most of us did not. The Nazis had planned and worked carefully. There was infiltration of both thought and people. Spies, collaborators and saboteurs were among us.

Because our house was the highest point in a flat land reaching toward the German border it was quickly commandeered as an artillery observation post. The guns were placed two miles further back. I quickly became involved. Riding my bicycle with my dogs accompanying me I did not attract attention as I gathered information from which military maps could be corrected for exact fixes of strategic points. Sometimes I would borrow the commander's horse for these expeditions but mostly I cycled. If Dash or Belco got too tired they would jump into a box on my carrier and ride with their front paws on my shoulders.

The infantry soon followed the artillery. About 12,000 strong men took up positions on our grounds and surrounding properties. By then I had more Bouviers. All ran freely except four grown ones that were posted at strategic points.

Trenches were quickly dug, some without consideration of water levels despite my cautions. These were soon waist deep in water. Other units respected my knowledge of our grounds and their trenches were, by comparison, comfortable. The main network of trenches was only 25 yards from our house. A quarter mile further there was an antitank canal. Trees in the woods were cut two feet above the ground leaving another tank barrier.

The first floor of our house was reinforced with, first, a layer of tree trunks and then sand bags. Branches and thickets were employed as camouflage for machine gun emplacements and ammunition storage units. Infantrymen were billeted in civilian homes in the village. Two officers lived in our house.

Three men were on duty at each post on a 24 hour watch. The sentries all wanted the help of a dog or puppy, especially during the night watches. No one could come near a Bouvier on sentry duty without the warning of a low growl or nudge. Sleepy soldiers were alerted to the approach of the watch officer on his rounds.

The rolling kitchens, still drawn by horses, were used to feed the men. Each company had its mess call eagerly answered by our Bouviers. They would stand at attention waiting for their share of the chow.

We needed coal for heat and cooking but there were no more deliveries. We improvised a sled and harnessed my dogs to go to the village for supplies. Zulma, our white donkey, refused to move and just sat down!

On May 11, 1940, everyone owning a car was requisitioned to evacuate the old and the sick. When I presented myself I was assigned to go with the secretary of the Town Hall and take the archives of the village to a secret vault in Antwerp. These were huge, leather bound books with brass fasteners. Luckily I had reinforced springs and heavy duty tires which, in peacetime had been used to absorb the weight of a trailer to bring grain from the docks. During scarcity, this stood in good stead when I had to drive in ploughed fields to avoid shell holes. All the chrome on the car had to be painted with a special blue paint. We also had to drive without lights during black-outs. On my return, when crossing the bridge in Wyneghem where I left the Secretary, I saw a plane in the canal. I proceeded home, alone with Belco.

It was three a.m. when I arrived home with Belco as bodyguard. There were many difficulties as the password to go through the lines had been changed. Several times I was challenged by a sentry pointing his rifle with fixed bayonet. It was a very uncomfortable feeling, especially when I could see a nervous, shaky hand on the trigger. After only two hours' rest I was ordered to leave for the coast as the bridge between was mined and scheduled for demolition.

There is hardly anything more fun than being a Bouvier pup. This du Clos des Cerberes fellow believes the world was put here for him to enjoy. Later he will learn about and assume responsibilities. The Flemish bakery cart asks for a bit of understanding. The dog is so hitched that he can help push—but it would seem he could, if inclined, just keep pace. Certainly his presence would deter swipers of sweets while the baker is away making deliveries. Puppy photo by Howard Kling. Cart photo from the collection of the late Janet W. Mack.

My mother and I hastily loaded the car and trailer with mattresses and blankets. I also took my bicycle. Later it was my only means of transportation. We also included a good supply of eggs. We left another 2,000 eggs for the stationed army as their supplies were overdue.

I chose Belco to accompany us. Dash was getting older and the younger ones had not had as much training or experience.

When we arrived at my sister's house in Antwerp the cook told us the family had already gone to La Panne on the coast. Bombs were already falling. We left some of our silverware, prefering a good supply of eggs. We took a large supply of gasoline in cans which had been brought from the tanks for us. My brother-in-law was manager for the Atlantic Refining Company in most countries in Europe. He had ordered large supplies of sugar to be dumped in the tanks at the approach of the German army. This would not only make the gas useless for refueling their tanks but it would jam the motors of their vehicles.

The slow exodus to the coast took nearly two days for what was normally only about three hours' drive. The roads were blocked by army and civilian traffic. Refugees were in all conditions. They moved by car, bicycle, wheelbarrow and on foot, besides anything on wheels that would move. Ghent already had been bombed and there was no room anywhere. We drove through the iron gates of the château. We introduced ourselves and begged for a night's lodging. Belco and some eggs, a rare commodity then, were an "Open Sesame" as they were often to be on our long journey.

We rejoined some of the family at the coast. Then we were ordered to move to France. Our point of entry had been closed.

After some arrangements we joined the Bell Telephone Company convoy ordered to Paris with their special equipment. When crossing the border I ordered Belco to hide under the mattress to avoid further delay with customs. French troops on the crossroads separated us from the rest of the convoy so we about did a "tour" of France; Calais, Abbeville and Dunkirk were included. We had to keep taking shelter, whenever possible, from planes dive-bombing or machine-gunning the civilians. At one time going bumper to bumper along a lane bordered by trees on one side, open fields on the other, we jumped out of the car leaving Belco to guard it. We ran toward a cluster of trees and landed in a manure heap. Returning to our car we saw many people walking about in dazed condition. One young couple held their dead baby in their arms. They heard crying and stopped. There was another baby beside its dead parents. After some hesitation the couple exchanged babies.

We headed for Clermont-Ferrand where we had friends. Our car was impounded and we spent three weeks there. We hid our trailer, supply of gasoline and tools in the garage of our friends' summer cottage. During this period I kept busy. Depending upon my bicycle for transportation and Belco for protection I tried to help the refugees who were arriving in most pitiful conditions. The Germans came closer and closer until they were in Vichy, just three miles away. Luckily for us the Germans stopped there to enjoy the wines and champagne. That gave us a few hours to get away.

Refugees were ordered to remain where they were but I was afraid to encounter the Germans and I had better reason to fear them than I knew then. I found out much later that our tenant farmer had betrayed me and that there was a price for my capture.

Always the Bouvier booster, Miss Bowles here donned an authentic Flemish milkmaid costume, hitched her great favorite, Ch. Marius du Clos des Cerberes, to a cart and got their photo in one of America's great newspapers. Philadelphia Evening Bulletin photo.

Smuggling is an ancient profession. Almost as old is the device of training a dog to carry the booty across the border. Belgian customs officials countered by training *their* Bouviers to contravene the canine contraband carriers. At the Valley Forge show in 1953 Miss Bowles, in an authentic customs uniform of 1900, demonstrated both facets of this training. Loaded with tobacco Ch. Marius did the smuggler dog crawl. His kennelmate, Ch. Ellydria, "captured" him. Photo by Shafer.

The leaving was difficult and dangerous. From our cache I took two heavy cans of gasoline and strapped them onto my bicycle. Belco helped me push the load up the hill and I brazenly "liberated" our car.

I hurried back to the châlet where I made inquiries how best to get out of town. It was important that we discipline ourselves against panic. We waited until dark before loading up. I had become a familiar sight with my bike and my dog but this was a different matter. Every detail had to be anticipated. The policeman on duty that night was paid to look the other way. We had to cross the mountains by moonlight. The route over Mount Dore, 6,000 feet up, was by a narrow, winding road.

Traveling without lights we headed for Perigueus on the way to Bordeaux. At that port on the southwestern coast of France we hoped to rejoin my sister, her husband and daughter. Cars were abandoned everywhere along our route. Some were wrecked. Many had become totally useless when they had consumed their last drop of gasoline.

We hoped to be in time to board the Manhattan for the last trip from France to the United States. But enroute we were told the Germans had surrounded Bordeaux. We selected Bayonne as our best alternative. It is the next furthermost town on the Bay of Biscay. We again went east for a visa to Cahors, an ancient Roman town. There we found more confusion, people shouting and pushing. Officials at the headquarters pushed everyone out of the building.

I went to the back of the building and crawled in through a window. Then I stood calmly at the desk. Because I was so calm it was assumed I belonged. When the post commander arrived I was able to depart quickly.

I had left my mother in the car with Belco. Even during what must have been a time of great stress for him a man felt he had to stop for a moment. He said: "Oh, a Bouvier. I owe my life to a Bouvier in World War I. I was left for dead in the trenches. The medics, accompanied by a Bouvier passed me over. They found no sign of life but the Bouvier insisted. On the chance the dog was right they took me into the medical station. That was twenty years ago."

After many more adventures and urged by the peril of our situation we reached Bayonne. As usual there were no accommodations available. The French had signed an armistice. That seemed only to create more confusion, if such was possible. We had to sleep in the car, my

European photographer DIM has captured Bouvier intensity and character in this head study of Dalila de la Fontaine au Roy. This daughter of Whist de Bois des Saules out of Youlande des Coudreaux was whelped in January 1956 and was a winner in Paris and elsewhere.

Miss Bowles walks her Roland du Clos des Cerberes in the snow at the entrance to Belco Farm.

Ch. Chef de Truffle became an important winner and sire for Miss Bowles. He was bred by Joan Butts (Ch. Coquin de la Thudinie—Ch. Draga de la Thudinie). He is pictured here as he won best of breed at Westminster in 1962. Photo by Brown.

mother on the front seat, Belco and I on the back seat. I was awakened from an uneasy sleep by Belco on the attack. He lept to the front seat and grabbed a man pointing a revolver at my mother. There was another man on the other side of the car. I never saw two men run so fast! We would not have been the first casualties of plunderers in those lawless days.

We had to remain in the Pyrenees for 18 months. Food was extremely short and we had to exist on 900 calories a day. It was during this period that Belco again saved my life. While cycling on a mountain road an oncoming truck, loaded with overhanging bags, swerved onto my side of the road leaving me barely a foot between it and a drop over the edge. I laid flat on the handlebars. Belco was leashed at my right. By pulling as hard as he could he kept me from falling under the wheels of the truck. The truck went on, leaving me in a heap on the road. Belco helped me home.

Finally, after three months in Portugal, we were able to embark for America. We arrived safely in May of 1942.

Belco and I gave training exhibitions for Dogs for Defense. We helped to train trainers for the Coast Guard's K-9 Corps. The Coast Guard had obtained the fine female, Ch. Lisa. From her Belco sired puppies for Dogs for Defense. Further, he and Lisa helped to raise funds for the program by pulling carts with collection boxes.

Belco died when he was 12 years old, brave and loyal to the end. I had him embalmed and brought him here to Collegeville, Pa. That was more than twenty years ago. We named our place Belco Farm.

We were never reimbursed for the military occupation and damage to our home in Belgium. What was not demolished by V-bombs was stolen. I had had a price on my head but thanks to Belco we were always a step ahead of the advancing German army. They searched for me to the end. I lost everything I owned except Belco. He lives on through his descendents, never forgotten.

SOME AMERICAN KENNELS

Blueberry Bank Kennels

THERE was no blaring of trumpets, no roll of drums to celebrate the arrival of the first Bouviers in the United States. The first dogs may have come here with returning World War I doughboys. If so there seems to be no record of their residence here. Certainly they had no lasting impact on Bouvier history in America.

Of those Bouviers arriving in the late 20's and the 30's there are some bare facts as represented in the AKC records of their registrations. The owners are mostly gone or untraceable. Show records don't tell us much because there were few entries. Because it was almost impossible to find competition in the breed, owners of the time usually found dog shows a zestless exercise. Such was the experience of Mrs. Virginia de Rochemont, one of the very few people of that era who still has an interest in Bouviers and vivid recollections of the dogs she and her family has enjoyed since the late 30's.

In the 1930's and 40's Louis de Rochemont was a very busy and influential man. He was the driving force behind Pathe Movietone News and he was a cofounder of the March of Time. In pre-television days these were two of the world's most important opinion molders. Newsreels were a part of every movie program and the March of Time in its movie and radio versions had a virtual monopoly on dramatization of the news.

This is Louis de Rochemont's account of how he and Virginia de Rochemont came to be pioneer Bouvier owners and breeders in the United States. "At the age of three our son, Louis de Rochemont III, was diagnosed as diabetic. His doctor told us: 'Listen, you must get a dog for this child.'

"We turned to my brother Richard for advice, as he was then the dog lover and owner in our family. Richard was living in France where he had Bouviers and he procured for us and shipped a trained female Bouvier we called Rita. She at once took charge of young Louie. She slept with him. He was subject to insulin shock. Whenever he began to wiggle and waggle she would come into our room and wake us. We always kept orange juice ready and, with Rita's warnings we were, time after time, able to keep the child from going into a coma.

```
LUMINA RITA, LOSH 86108, female, whelped Mar. 26, 1937, Breeder - J. Josis

                    Demosthene, LOSH 36211       Bolton, LOSH 36208
                    Freton, LOSH 52949           Lidiane, LOSH 27904
                    Rita, property of M. G. Carette   Unknown
          Cleps de la Ville des Doges, LOSH 52960     Unknown
                    Doudou du Grand Marais, LOSH 36162   Bruno de Rebecq, LOSH 28646
                    Franchette, LOSH 47280       Viviane, LOSH 36162
                    Esperance de la Roselle, LOSH 40390   Bolton, LOSH 35208
                                                 Viviane, LOSH 36162

LUMINA RITA, LOSH 86108

                    Stop du Genie, LOSH 18068    Brillant, LOSH 12939
                    As du Prefeuillet, LOSH 23832    Sora de Ramillies, LOSH 9586
                    Olivette de la Lys, LOSH 19383   Goliath de la Lys, LOSH 13021
          Herbolette du Prefeuillet, LOSH 54890       Dinah de la Lys, LOSH 13281
                    Stop du Genie, LOSH 18068    Brillant, LOSH 12939
                    Ottara, LOSH 54703           Sora de Ramillies, LOSH 9586
                    Corona, LOSH 48350           Triumph de Pont-a-Rieu, LOSH 19905
                                                 Sara, owned by M.E. Decroes
```

"Lumina Rita, our first Bouvier, was whelped in 1937. Since she was already trained when she came to us that must have been in 1938. We bought our best Bouvier, a fine big, gray fellow, Czardas van het Bunderbosh, just before the Nazis marched into Holland. He had been judged 'the Queen's champion' and he came to us on the last Dutch ship to sail for New York. Strangely, we did not get the bill for him until after V-E Day."

Other importations followed the war. Virginia de Rochemont became interested in breeding. There was one litter of 16 but all did not survive. A number of Bouvier puppies were bestowed upon appreciative friends. One even went to movie mogul Jack Warner, the man whose earliest successes were Rin Tin Tin pictures. A de Rochemont Bouvier appeared in the film, "Outward Bound."

Like Evert van de Pol on the west coast, the de Rochemonts plan

Family portrait is of Ch. Aurega du Clos des Cerberes winning the brood bitch class at the specialty in 1968. Aurega's on the left with George Edge. Altaire and Bunji were nine month old pups. At middle left is Aurega when she went BOS at the '67 specialty. Zorina du Clos des Cerberes, right, was the second bitch to win a west coast show title. Imported Ch. Remando's Katleen, bottom left, and her daughter, Ch. Elaine du Clos des Cerberes, right, were also outstanding producers. All photos except Zorina by Gilbert.

to resume breeding Bouviers. When they were interviewed Virginia de Rochemont said: "Bouviers are right for these times. They are the kind of dog people want and need today."

De Rochemont added: "We love all dogs but we think Bouviers are especially wonderful. We plan to breed them again. Our kennels at our New Hampshire home, Blueberry Bank, are nearly ready and I've made inquiries to obtain new breeding stock."

Among the breeds in the United States during World War II Bouviers must have had the highest per capita enlistment in the Dogs for Defense program. De Rochemont Bouviers also served in the Coast Guard.

Du Clos des Cerberes

In the previous chapter Miss Edmee Bowles told the story of flight from her European home just ahead of the Nazis—and of how she, her mother and her Bouvier, Belco, arrived in the United States and made their home in Collegeville, Pa.

A man from the Philadelphia area, Commander Newbolt Ely, was placed in charge of the Coast Guard's war dog program. For him Miss Bowles trained both dogs and trainers. So she could also breed Bouviers for the Dogs for Defense program she obtained a bitch, Lisa, from George Young of New Canaan, Conn. Lisa was a daughter of the first AKC Bouvier champion, Boojar van Westergoo, a Dutch import.

Early in 1958 Miss Bowles purchased Wandru des Coudreaux from France. In 1960 she imported Remado's Katleen from Belgium. Then she bought Chef de Truffe from Robert and Joan Butts of Springfield, Ill. These became the du Clos des Cerberes foundation dogs. From them has come a long line of obedience and show winning Bouviers—and many more that were successful as family companions.

Chef de Truffe (Coquin de la Thudinie - Draga de la Thudinie finished his championship title with a five point major and 23 points. He was nine times best of breed from the classes. His sire had 30 group placements including one first—often showing under judges who had never before seen a top quality Bouvier.

Belco and Ch. Lisa produced Ch. Marius du Clos des Cerberes, one of Miss Bowles' all time favorites. He was the Westminster best of breed each year, 1945-50. He was also a group placer. Miss Bowles had bought Ch. Ellydria from Evert van de Pol. Bred to her he pro

The five points she won as best of winners at the ABFC's first specialty in 1965 went a long way toward Del-Poppy du Clos de Cerberes' AKC show title. Club co-founder Carl May presented the trophy. Owner Mrs. Carrie Adell was prideful. Handler Pat Maremann watched the photographer and the late Albert Van Court, who judged, held the ribbons.
Photo by Gilbert.

At the ABFC specialty held in conjunction with the Westchester show in September, 1971 Jasper du Clos des Cerberes went from the open male class over all of the champions present to best of breed.
Photo by Shafer.

duced Bel Ami du Clos des Cerberes. Bel Ami sired seven champions including Ch. Sapho du Clos des Cerberes.

Through all the years the unquenchable Miss Bowles has been an imaginative and active press agent for Bouviers. She either made or imported costumes and other props which were used in photographs that won Bouviers space in newspapers and magazines all over North America.

Miss Bowles' Bouviers continue to win. In 1971 Ch. Jaspar du Clos des Cerberes went from the open dog class past all the champions competing to win the American Bouvier des Flandres Club's annual specialty show. A homebred, he's by Ch. Altair du Clos des Cerberes out of Brabo du Clos des Cerberes.

In 1972 Miss Bowles imported Tania du Posty Arlequin, then in whelp to Sim de Bronchain. She has, at this writing, great hopes for all of the litter of eight—and especially for the two which she kept. Miss Bowles is always seeking new challenges—and better Bouviers.

Madrone Ledge

Ray and Marion Hubbard had had Saint Bernards, Poodles, an Irish Wolfhound and a Bedlington Terrier. They were visiting San Francisco's Golden Gate show in 1953 when they had their first real encounter with a Bouvier. They were captivated by the combination of gentleness, character and authority. The dog on the bench was being exhibited by Bouvier pioneer Evert van de Pol—and they sought him out and purchased Cere Bere, a bitch by Bonaparte v. Darling-Astrid.

Cere Bere didn't know enough about automobiles and highways. She was killed in 1957. Later the Hubbards replaced her. Through Miss Janet Mack they imported a three-month-old bitch, Krepsie de la Thudinie. She became the first Bouvier to win an AKC championship on the west coast in 15 years. Krepsie was a pale silver with a black mask. Her kennel name, Flax, was descriptive. At that time the Hubbards were still living in Ross, California. There was a degree of frustration in showing Bouviers on the west coast at that time due to a dearth of breed competition. Only Mrs. Dorothy Stern of Goleta, Calif., with two dogs (one from Evert van de Pol and a Dutch import) was providing competition.

The Hubbards bought Beiard D'l'Vons. Bred to Krepsie he sired a litter of fawns and light brindles.

In 1965 Madrone Ledge moved to Sands Point, Long Island. A year later the Hubbards imported the littermates, Pebbles du Posty Arlequin and Pepita du Posty Arlequin. Both completed AKC show titles.

In 1966 Mrs. Hubbard, with help from Miss Mack, rescued Grenadier Coquette of Walden from a girls' school where she had been given temporary shelter when abandoned. She was one of two puppies whelped in 1962 by the then ten-year-old Coquette de la Thudinie. The dam was a litter sister to Ch. Coquin de la Thudinie that had been imported by the Butts of Springfield, Ill. Grenadier Coquette of Walden first went to Mrs. Hubbard, Sr. on the west coast and it was there she won her AKC title.

Chet Collier of Irvington-on-Hudson, N.Y. bought Coquette and began showing her, along with his Madrone Ledge Blazen.

In 1967 Marion Hubbard attended Belgium's Charleroi dog show. She came home with Odelette du Posty Arlequin and word of a spectacular dog named "Naris."

In 1968 Ray Hubbard toured Belgium kennels. Shortly afterwards he purchased Picolette du Posty Arlequin. Odelette became the top winning Bouvier bitch in 1968 and 1969 and won the largest specialty in 1969 under the noted Belgian breeder and judge Victor Martinage. In 1971 Picolette became the first bitch to win the working group and a best in show. She also won the ABFC National Specialty at Philadelphia.

Madrone Ledge Socrate, at two years of age, became the first American-bred Bouvier to win a best in show. The following weekend he added best of breed at the 1971 Specialty in Philadelphia.

Ray and Marion Hubbard share in the challenge of breeding, training and showing better and better Bouviers. Their energies and devotion to the breed are, in appreciable measure, responsible for the Bouvier's healthy growth in North America.

Redfox Kennels

Life's greatest pleasures are often unplanned. In 1960 Carolyn and Charles Markham of Bartley, New Jersey bought their first Bouvier for companionship and as a measure of security in their automobile agency. Deewal Bonne Amie became much more than that. The daughter of Ch. Argus de la Thudinie-Ch. Deewal Nicole at her first show went from the puppy class to reserve winners bitch. She finished her championship before she was two years old.

Bred to Ch. Rostan du Clos des Cerberes she produced a litter of eleven. Of these three, Ch. Redfox Lariat CD, Ch. Redfox Velvet Lassie CD and Ch. Redfox Clonmel won a total of five AKC titles. By then the Markhams had enthusiastically undertaken the Bouvier challenge.

Carolyn Markham bred her Lassie to Ch. Picard des Preux Vuilbaard and kept a puppy she called Redfox Liberty Bell. He went on to become the first Bouvier to win American, Canadian and Mexican titles.

Clonmel was bred to Virginia de Rochemont's Jingles of Blueberry Bank in 1965. He produced Ch. Redfox Smokie, the first Bouvier to win American, Canadian and Bermudian CD's—and all with distinction.

The Markhams imported Ch. Quina de la Thudinie produced just one litter before she died of intestinal complications. From her litter by Lariat she produced Redfox Quina Tubbina. That was in 1967.

Ernest Topoliski of York, Pa. bred his Blandford's Bianca to Smokie. In that litter were Ch. Babka de Saint Roch and Ch. Babette de Saint Roch. In 1971 from imported Sia du Posty Arlequin Smokie produced Redfox Whisp of Smoke that won nine points before she was 17 months old and went on to reserve winners bitch at the 1971 specialty.

Meanwhile Carolyn Markham's commitment to Bouviers had been expanding beyond that of owner, breeder, exhibitor and obedience trainer. She had hired a professional handler the first time she had shown Bonne Amie. In 1967 the AKC licensed her as a "limited handler" after an apprenticeship under W. Harry Manning.

Kennel names hopefully become something of a breeder's trademark. Sometimes they are capriciously chosen. Sometimes they find their origins in foreign languages—as with French and Bouviers. These can be difficult to spell and even more difficult to remember. The Markhams chose Redfox for reasons beyond its distinctness and rememberability. They had shown horses for some years before dis-

Ch. Redfox Lariat CD was a homebred. Sired by Ch. Rostan du Clos des Cerberes, he was out of Ch. Deewal Bonne Amie. The judge in this photo is James W. Case and the handler W. Harry Manning.
All photos by Gilbert.

Redfox Clonmel was just past his second birthday when he completed his show title at the Mid-Hudson show in July 1965. Maxwell Riddle judged and W. Harry Manning handled.

Ch. Deewal Bonne Amie (Ch. Argus de la Thudinie - Deewal Nicole) established herself as the matriach of Redfox Kennels in Flanders, N.J. On this Feb. 1965 day in Hartford owner Carolyn Markham handled and Frank Foster Davis judged.

Ch. Quina de la Thudinie was photographed winning three points at Bucks County in 1969 just six weeks after whelping 14 puppies. Mrs. Charles G. Markham, co-owner of Redfox Kennels handled. The judge was Henry Stoecker.

covering Bouviers. Redfox was their fabulous open jumper that competed until he was 33 and lived to the age of 36.

Blandford Kennel

In recent years one of the strongest Bouvier forces in the midwest has been the Blandford kennel of Agnes and Pat Miller in Mt. Clemens, Mich.

Blandford's foundation stud and top winning show dog was Ch. Boris van de Ouden Dijk, imported from Miss Julia Van Vorst of The Netherlands. "Nikki's" winnings in the midwest were important steps in helping Bouviers become better known in that part of the country. In 1968 he was the top winning Bouvier in Canadian shows, the best in the stud dog class at the ABFC specialty in 1969. The latter is a competition where a sire is shown with his get—and Nikki sired many winners before his death in 1971. One son, Blandford's Raoel, was, at 13 months, the youngest Bouvier to win both American and Canadian championships. Raoel was also the 1969 second-ranking Bouvier in Canadian shows and best of opposite sex (to best of breed) at the 1969 ABFC specialty.

A Blandford bred Bouvier was the first to win a Canadian show. Ch. Blandford's Basko, owned by Mr. and Mrs. Harry Dyk of Norlock Kennels, Kleinburg, Ontario, won the 1972 Canadian National Sportsmen's show. He's by Nikki out of Penny the Pooh.

Des Preux Vuilbaards Kennel

The 120 or more breeds recognized by the AKC are such a diverse lot that there is a pure-bred dog for almost every conceivable human taste and need. Even within Bouviers there is opportunity for a wide range of opinion and expression through ownership, breeding, training and in show and obedience competitions.

Robert Abady of Des Preux Vuilbaards Kennel is an individualist with strong opinions on many subjects—and especially on Bouviers. Like the Europeans he believes Bouviers should be attack trained. He sees the Bouvier as a law and order adjunct. In a controversial *Sports Illustrated* article he was quoted as saying it takes about a year to train his Bouviers to attack and that he selects only the most stable dogs for this work.

This homebred brother-sister combination became double holders of AKC titles. Ch. Redfox Lariat CD and Ch. Redfox Lassie CD had this double win at Westminster in 1967 under Judge Peter Knoop. Lariat was best of breed and Lassie winners bitch. Carolyn Markham handled.

Ch. Giaconda du Clos des Cerberes was best of opposite sex at the ABFC specialty in 1965. Pat Marcmann handled for owner Carl B. May, Jr. Both photos by Shafer.

If the success of Abady's breeding program was measured only by the success of Des Preux Vuilbaards Bouviers on the bench—admittedly a standard some might be expected to reject—the record would be outstanding.

Abady was born in Curacao, the Dutch West Indies. At 21 he traveled to Germany and Holland. There he first came to know the Bouvier des Flandres. In 1963 he bought his first Bouviers and settled on a Quebec farm. Later he became discouraged with his stock, discarded what he had and moved to Stormville, N. Y. For breeding stock to meet his high standards he traveled to Belgium. There he bought Nota du Posty Arlequin and two other bitches. His great triumph, however, was the acquisition of Ch. Marc de la Thudinie. Justin Chastel is quoted as calling Marc the greatest dog he ever owned. Marc was best in show at both Brussels and Charleroi. He continued his winning ways in the U.S. but it was as a stud that he made his greatest contributions here.

For Abady Nota produced the outstanding winner and sire, Ch. Prudhon des Preux Vuilbaards. Among his many winning get are Ch. Hanover's Alon and Ch. Hanover's Ardanne, owned by Dr. Clifford and Joyce Bodarky.

Abady is an artist and student of nutrition. He has established a business in nutritional supplements for dogs. Recently he and his wife, Isobel, moved to Verbank, N.Y.

Bibarcy Kennels, Reg.

Art and Mary Pedersen were well indoctrinated in dog breeding and dog shows when they first welcomed a Bouvier into their home. Bibarcy's first winners were Collies. Soon after they added Miniature Schnauzers. Their Collie bitch, Bibarcy's Blueberry a la Mode was not only best in show quality, she did win a show.

The Pedersens bought their first Bouvier for their son in 1964 but she failed to survive an outbreak of encephalitis. Being dog-wise they knew the right time to buy a puppy is when the right puppy is available. At Deewal Kennels they reserved a puppy from Ch. Deewal Argusette by Ch. Job de la Thudinie.

Their patience paid off. Bibarcy's Job's Daughter became the top producing Bouvier dam in AKC history. Eight of her whelps wor

Ranking twelfth all-time in AKC shows is Canadian and American Ch. Boris van de Ouden Dijk CD. He was photographed (top) by Gilbert as he, and his sons, Canadian and American Ch. Blanford Raoel and Ch. Blandford's Bolte, were shown by owners Pat and Agnes Miller as he won the stud dog class at the ABFC specialty in 1969. In the photo below of Ch. Blandford's Raoel it is easily seen what is meant by "desirable cobbiness" in Bouviers. Raoel was only 13 months old when he completed both American and Canadian show championships—probably the youngest Bouvier to attain both titles. He was best of opposite sex at the 1969 ABFC specialty.

Ch. Bibarcy's Soldat de Plomb's record is the most spectacular of American-bred Bouviers. The late Virgil Johnson selected him best in the Piedmont show in February 1972 with Houston Clark handling. At Council Bluffs in 1970 (above) with owners Dr. and Mrs. Arthur Pedersen handling Soldat was BOB and Bibarcy's Songuese was BOS. Photos by Lloyd W. Olson (top) and Earl Graham.

AKC show titles. Five came from one litter by Ch. Deewal Demon Ripp. The other three from a litter sired by Ch. Deewal Homer.

Job's Daughter's most spectacular scion is Ch. Bibarcy's Soldat de Plomb that in a short time won six bests in show. Plomb was the second American-bred Bouvier to win a show. He was the first dog of American-bred parents to do so.

A 1969 litter by Ch. Pebbles du Posty Arlequin - Ch. Bibarcy's Cassandra produced two more show titlists, Ch. Tambour de Ville and Ch. Bibarcy's Tourterelle. Also in 1969 the Pedersens imported Sadine du Posty Arlequin. She became an AKC champion in 1971.

For many years Dr. and Mrs. Pedersen maintained his practice, their home and kennels in Council Bluffs, Iowa. Their move to Gaffney, S.C. in 1971 established a Bouvier "beachhead" in the South.

Hilgrand Kennels, Reg.

Murray and Shirley Horowitz of North Woodmere on Long Island in New York registered their Hilgrand Kennels in 1967. Their foundation Bouviers were Ch. Deewal Hardiesse and Ch. Deewal Grand Prix. They bred Deewal Samantha, the first Bouvier to win an AKC sanctioned match at the Suffolk County Kennel Club in 1967. The Horowitzes declare Samantha was given the Deewal prefix as their tribute to the encouragement and assistance they had received from the late Dorothy Walsh.

Like most dedicated breeders the Horowitzes feel a greater sense of achievement when they can indoctrinate a new enthusiast into Bouvier ranks than they do when finishing an AKC championship on one of their own dogs. They brought Ralph and Sandi Goldman of South Salem, N.Y. into the Bouvier ranks when they sold them, as a puppy, Ch. Hilprize Kelli Sandra (Ch. Job de la Thudinie - Ch. Deewal Hardiesse). The Goldmans, in turn, bred Ch. Vlaanderen's I'm Kelli Too (Ch. Prudhon des Preux Vuilbaard - Ch. Hilprize Kelli.) Kelli Too is almost certainly the youngest Bouvier ever to attain an AKC championship. Whelped March 27, 1973, she finished at the Philadelphia show in stiff competition on Dec. 9, 1973. She was just 258 days old—or just a bit over 8½ months! It was an especially gratifying accomplishment for the Goldmans since the dam died shortly after giving birth.

At this writing the Horowitzes are actively showing their Ch. U

Oliver des Preux Vuilbaard (Ch. Noceur de la Thudinie - Taquine des Preux Vuilbaard) He has many best of breeds and six group placements to his credit. A show career represents quite a change of life-style for Oliver. Shirley Horowitz found a classified ad in a community newspaper offering a young adult Bouvier for sale. Curiosity prompted a phone call. It was explained the family could no longer keep their pet. When the Horowitzes heard the pedigree they had to see the dog. When they saw they bought.

Again at this writing, the Horowitzes have a Keeshond, Can. Ch. Paladin's Jolly Roger, on the show circuit and nearing his AKC title. They have also shown a Kuvasz bitch.

However, it is as scholars of all of dogdom that the Horowitzes are best known. Their cynological library is one of the most comprehensive and judiciously assembled in North America. Some of their prints, bronzes and other art pieces depicting Bouviers are pictured in the chapter on the Bouvier in Art.

Bras De Fer Kennels

Sometimes a first dog's successes will so infect his owners with "showitis" that their involvement and delights will grow and grow. That's the way it happened to Frank and Lil Mees of West Chester, Pa. The puppy they bought at Robert Abady's Des Preux Vuilbaards Kennel was too young to take home. When he arrived they named him Nic. It wasn't until his papers arrived that they discovered his registered name was to be Prudhon des Pruex Vuilbaards. That was in 1966.

Less than a year later at the Bouvier National Specialty in Philadelphia Nic, at 13 months, went from the American-bred class all the way to best of winners—over Odelette, the winner in the open bitch class and the rest of the class females—and over the winner of the open dog class. *And* the winner of the open dog class that day was an import with considerable potential—Naris de la Thudinie. The judge was the late Albert E. Van Court.

In July 1968 Vuilbaard offered Frank Mees a bitch that was failing her opportunities as a brood bitch. They bought the Ch. Job de la Thudinie bitch. Oriane, a fawn. After patient treatment for a low-grade vaginal infection they bred her to Nic. Oriane has since pro-

This head study of Genadier Aleida of River Oakes CD might be used to illustrate many desirable factors such as character, intensity, careful grooming, proper ear set and trim and coat quality. Aleida was owned and trained by Virginia Bull of New Jersey.

Ch. Ripeau Bras de Fer is owned by Mr. and Mrs. Jay Arnold of Northfield, N.J. Although not bred by Vuilbaard she's from Vuibaard stock which in this instance is three-quarter Chastel. She's by Prudhon out of Orianne. Photo by Gilbert.

Ch. Picard des Preux Vuilbaards is by Marc de la Thudinie out of Nota de la Thudinie—and that makes him a full brother to Ch. Prudhon des Preux Vuilbaards. Photo by Gilbert.

Ch. Ur des Preux Vuilbaards is owned by Mr. and Mrs. Fred Joyner of Ft. Tobacco, Md.

duced several outstanding litters. In her first was Ch. Ripeau Bras de Fer owned by Mr. and Mrs. Jay Arnold of Northfield, N.J.

Until Naris passed him, Nic was the winningest Bouvier in AKC history. He had 93 best of breeds, eight group firsts and 29 additional group placements. Five of his get are already champions and, at this writing, more are nearing their titles.

A Nic daughter, Ch. Bougie de Feu Allure, owned by Mr. and Mrs. Walter Herec of Detroit, won her title at the age of nine months. (That was the record until her half-sister (via Nic), Ch. Vlaanderen's I'm Kelli Too, shaved some weeks off it by finishing at 258 days.) Considering the strength of any AKC working group it is amazing that Allure was also a group placer at 11 months of age.

There can be no conclusion other than that Nic's daughters have shown their quality young. His Ch. Tamara Bras de Fer was the first American bred bitch—and the second, imported or U.S. bred—to win a working group. She was only 22 months old at the time of that triumph.

Bras de Fer Bouviers are noted for toplines, temperament and type. They are always formidable show ring competition.

A son of Nic's, Ch. Duxbury House's Ulrich, went all the way from the junior puppy class to best of winners at the December 1971 specialty. He now heads the Bras de Fer Kennel and the Mees can project a continuing line of first rank Bouviers.

Deewal Kennels, Reg.

> *Editor's note: This is the corner into which the author painted herself when she undertook the labors of writing a much-needed book on Bouviers. No "Complete Bouvier" book could be complete without a history of Deewal Kennels, but the author is the owner of Deewal. Her aunt and uncle, Fred and Dorothy Walsh, made her heir to the AKC registered name because they were confident she would carry on very much in their own style and manner.*
>
> *As an author writing about Deewal none of her alternatives were attractive. She could have affected an insincere humility about what Fred and Dorothy Walsh achieved as importers, as exhibitors, as breeders, as Bouvier boosters,*

Ch. Deewal Hardiesse was the first show titlist for the Hilgrand, Reg. kennel of Dr. Murray and Shirley Horowitz of Valley Stream, N.Y. Photo by Gilbert.

Picking from this litter of ten was very nearly a sure thing. Five of these puppies became AKC show Champions, making Ch. Bibarcy's Job's Daughter the top producing dam for 1969. The sire was Deewal Demon Ripp. The owners are Dr. Art and Mary Pedersen of Bibarcy.

Ch. Biarcy's Casanova is another of Bibarcy's prides. Owned by Dr. Art and Mary Pedersen, he was bred by William A. Pedersen.

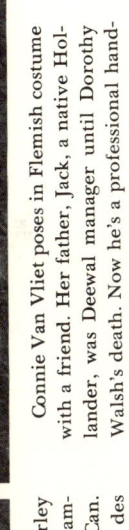

A homebred at the Hanover Farms Kennels of Dr. Clifford and Joyce Bodarky is Ch. Hanover's Ardanne. She's by Ch. Prudhon des Preux Vuilbaards-Ch. Sarita du Clos des Cerberes. George Edge handled her.

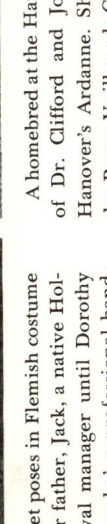

Connie Van Vliet poses in Flemish costume with a friend. Her father, Jack, a native Hollander, was Deewal manager until Dorothy Walsh's death. Now he's a professional handler from his Plateau Kennel in New Jersey.

Ch. Delanda's Nemo, with Ms. Shirley Landa, was DeLanda's first, and biggest champion. Reported to be 150 pounds, he's by Can. Ch. Frisia's Bob out of Nanay du Clos des Cerberes.

> as sportsman and sportswoman and as responsible citizens of the canine community. She could have attempted objectivity about a subject in which she has a deep personal involvement—and that is obviously impossible. Or, she could have just plain bragged on her own.
>
> None of the above happened. I've written the Deewal section in this chapter. And now objectivity demands that I report I met Fred Walsh once, just long enough for a handshake. The same for Dorthy Walsh and the author. Argus de la Thudinie is a different matter. The one time I saw him he was in a working group ring at a show near Reading, Pa. With his presence and his quality he demanded and got the group first. I didn't believe any judge could have missed him. The BIS judge, a testy AKC director, wavered—then gave the show to a Poodle handled by Ann Hone Rogers.
>
> That one experience made an Argus fan of me so I won't pretend objectivity when writing about him. H. D.

Louis de Rochemont gave the Bouvier "fever" to Fred and Dorothy Walsh. In 1943 he gave them a Bouvier named Max. Their conversion into Bouvier boosters had begun but its completion would take nearly a decade. A next, and logical, step was to acquire a companion for Max. Appropriately she was named Lassie. The pair led a happy existence as farm and cattle dogs at the Walsh's residence near Cambridge, Md.

The family moved to Croton, N.J. There Poodles and Quarter Horses became their absorbing interest—but Bouvier fascination was building. In 1952 the horse barns were converted into kennels and Bouviers were cast in starring roles. Dorothy Walsh continued breeding and showing the Poodles but it was undeniably Bouvier time at Deewal.

Serious Bouvier breeding at Deewal began with the purchase from Evert van de Pol of Bonaparte von Darling Astrid, one of the early American show champions. He'd been bred in Holland by H.L.M. Veugulers. From the de Rochemont Blueberry Bank Kennels came a gray and black bitch, Wallonne (Polox - Beeta van Wakershof.) AKC records show a litter from this mating whelped on June 10, 1948.) Wallonne was mated to Miss Bowles' Ch. Marius du Clos des

For many years Fred and Dorothy Walsh were found in the Bouvier benching area during Westminster time. This photo was taken in the basement of the old Garden in 1960. Ch. Argus de la Thudinie attended Dorothy Walsh while Deewal Nicole directed her Bouvier charm at Fred Walsh.

An airview dramatizes the scope of Deewal under Fred and Dorothy Walsh. In the center foreground is the kennel. Nearby is the home of kennel manager Jack Van Vliet. Note the enviable acreage under fence.
Photo by Stephanie Rancou.

For many years Dorothy Walsh put her abilities and her energies into popularizing Bouviers. She wrote thousands of letters to people who inquired about Bouviers, made innumerable phone calls and became a dynamic center of Bouvier activity.

Cerberes and they produced Deewal Yhelot. She was bred to Miss Bowles' Bel Ami du Clos des Cerberes. The Walshes campaigned a pup from the resultant litter and she became Ch. Deewal Zita. Bonaparte's only champion for Deewal came from Zita—Ch. Deewal Toronto.

Fred H. Walsh was a decisive man. Bouviers were so few in North America that there was little choice of breeding stock. Like the good advertising man that he was, Walsh researched the problem. He gathered all of the material he could about the European kennels and their Bouviers. He decided to go to the Belgian route.

He imported Argus de la Thudinie that had won first prizes at Binche, Warve, Ypres, Vieux-Dieu and Brussels. Walsh was able to buy him because he was nearly eight years old and because he had been widely enough used at stud in Belgium that his blood was abundantly available there. In an era when it was a brave group judge who would give a Bouvier a good look Argus averaged a group placement every six weeks during his active career here.

Walsh imported Faussette l'Ideal de Charleroi, a prize winner at Brussels, Warve and Lille because he felt she would make a good nick with Argus. Hardy l'Ideal de Charleroi and Irca de la Thudinie also made the trans-Atlantic trip to Deewal. All became AKC Champions except Hardy. He sired eight AKC show titlists. Argus had seven AKC champions in a shorter stud career in the U.S. One of his AKC champion sons, Erlo de la Thudinie, had been whelped in Belgium in 1955.

Later the Walshes imported Argus' grandson, Hion de la Thudinie. He was a winning campaigner and sired seven AKC champions. After Hion came the Belgian champion, Ch. Job de la Thudinie, a top AKC producer with 13 champion get at this writing.

After a medical accident took Fred Walsh in 1963 Dorothy Walsh continued breeding activities with the help of Jack Van Vliet who was serving as Deewal's kennel manager. She imported Quiar de la Thudinie in 1970. Ch. Quiar won best of breed at the Westminister show in 1972 just before Mrs. Walsh passed away. At the September 1972 specialty, Quiar was selected best of opposite sex by another breed pioneer, Carl May, Jr.

It wasn't all breeding for show qualities and campaigning their Bouviers in the ring. The Walshes had far too much depth and social conscience for that. Through the years their pride was the service

When you are a youngster having a Bouvier puppy is like having your own live and playful Teddy Bear. Chari Raye McLean has always had Bouvier playmates. Now that she is entering young womanhood the author's daughter is an accomplished junior showman.

Chari, then nine, handled Deewal Calant Charlaire CD to BOB while mom handled Deewal Lucette to BOS at the Pasadena KC. Cevon McLean was ten when he won a novice award in showmanship with Deewal Calant at the Santa Ana show in 1970. The McLean children won over 15 showmanship ribbons with patient Calant. Photos by Bill Francis and Alfred Stillman.

Deewal-bred and Deewal-donated Bouviers were giving to the blind. The Walshes worked with The Guiding Eyes for the Blind at Yorktown Heights, N. Y.

At Deewal adaptability and suitability for service to the blind was at least as important a breeding consideration as show conformation. At this writing 36 Deewal Bouviers have survived Guiding Eyes' stringent screening process, have successfully mastered the training program—and have served as eyes for the unsighted.

Ch. Deewal Argusue CD was the highest scoring dog in an obedience trial among 185 dogs. The AKC's highest obedience degree is Utility Dog. The first Bouvier to attain it was Deewal Merveille.

Deewal has bred more than 45 AKC show champions at this writing and it is certain the figure will be appreciably higher before publication.

Deewal won the ABFC specialty in 1966, 1967 and 1974 with, respectively, Ch. Job de la Thudinie, Ch. Deewal Lorenzo and Deewal Victor.

In addition to membership in the American Bouvier des Flandres Club Dorothy and Fred Walsh belonged to the Societe Royale de Saint Hubert and the Club National Belge du Bouvier des Flandres in France.

Deewal's proudest moment came when the American Bouvier des Flandres Club voted to offer a challenge trophy in honor of Dorothy Walsh.

Deewal Kennels have a new home now, in the rolling Pennsylvania hills near Chester Springs. There Lt. Col. Charles G. and Claire McLean continue to breed, to import, to train, to exhibit and to boost Bouviers.

Hanover Farm Kennels

Although the Hanover Farm Kennels of Dr. Clifford and Joyce Bodarky has been quite successful in breeding and campaigning show champions the Bodarkys feel obedience work is the natural forte of Bouviers. In recent years they have averaged better than one new CD per year, each of their own training and handling.

The Perkiomenville, Pa. establishment is home for Ch. Hanover's Alon, Ch. Hanover's Ardanne, Ch. Hanover's Beatrix, Ch. Hanover's Belle Amie, Ch. Hanover's Charleroi and Ch. Urex Bras de Fer. Dr. Bodarky says that what started in 1965 as limited hobby with the pur-

Ch. Zorra du Clos des Cerberes was whelped in June 1953 by Elfrida du Clos des Cerberes by Bel Ami du Clos des Cerberes. Marcus du Clos des Cerberes is not an AKC titlist but he's happy in a rural setting, the natural habitat of a Bouvier. He's owned by Mr. and Mrs. Richard Klausli of Lansing, Mich.

This was the kennel of Doris Stern, an early Bouvier fancier in California. Thankfully ears are now cropped more expertly and more easily than just a few years back. And with better results. Left to right: Duke van Young, Arendine v d Vlashoek, Murphy of Fair Hills, Bertha van Nessa and Charpie.

Virginia Bull was an early Bouvier s[upp]orter in the U.S. With her at left is Gre[na]dier Alieda of River Oakes CD. Above, [Ch.] U Oliver des Preux Vuilbaards has bee[n a] consistent group winner for the Horow[itz] Hilgrand Kennels. The late Alva Rosenb[erg] selected Ch. Picolette du Posty Arlequi[n as] the first Bouvier bitch to win an Ameri[can] show at Great Barrington in August, 19[ ]. Photos by Shafer (left) and Gilbert (below[).]

chase from Miss Edmee Bowles of Ch. Sarita du Clos des Cerberes and Liska du Clos des Cerberes CD has become an intensive and extensive undertaking. Both Bodarkys attribute a great part of their success to their emphasis on socialization. The ten or so adult dogs and the puppies all have freedom of access to the house and all of them spend their share of time in the house.

One distinguishing characteristic of breeders is optimism. Most have projections of their breeding programs for several generations ahead. They love the dogs they have but they thrive on their confidence they can do even better. The McLeans are no exception. They recently imported three Chastel-bred bitches, Silette, Valda and Vertu de la Thudinie. All have the genetic, personality and temperament factors the McLeans wish to emphasize. Vertu, however, has since been sold to Dr. and Mrs. Gerald Ginsberg of Abbington, Pa.

In a listing of this nature it is a virtual certainty that some who eminently deserve recognition are omitted. One factor regretted by the author might be called a generation gap. She did not have the opportunity of knowing most of the earlier breeders and exhibitors in the United States and Canada. Unfortunately it was not possible to contact all who are still living. However, it is hoped there will be a second edition of this book and an effort will be made to correct both errors and omissions.

A second edition of *The Complete Bouvier des Flandres* will certainly have to be much thicker if it is to introduce properly all of the Bouvier kennels which will be supporting growing breed popularity some five years hence.

Among the newer kennels which are already making a visible impact on Bouvier quality and popularity is that of Joyce Bodarky of Perkiomenville, Pa. and that of Ernest Topolski of York, Pa. who enjoys the multiple role of breeder, trainer, exhibitor and handler. Another is the La Grande Maison Kennel of John Milanovits in St. Louis, Mo. Mrs. Shirley Landa's kennel, De Landa's imported Terry du Posty Arlequin finished his AKC championship in near record time. On the west coast the Mission Bell Kennel of Mr. and Mrs. William Greer emphasizes equally competition in conformation and in obedience. They finished JezZaa Bell, the second Bouvier to win both a show title and a CD on the West Coast. The first was Deewal Beau Paquet, owned by Mr. and Mrs. Howard Welch. An early west coast breeder was Mrs. Christy Comer. It was she who from Madrone Ledge Blaise and Deewal Brutus bred JezZaa Bell.

There were good Bouviers in the United States in the pioneering days of the 30's as this photo of Julius Bliss' Inga and Astra proves. Taken in 1938 by an unidentified photographer, this double portrait captures the alertness and devotion which inspires intense breed loyalty among Bouvier owners. By Ch. Bojar van Westergoo out of Lariane, Inga and Astra were litter sisters to Caprice. Bliss thought it appropriate that a member of the socially prominent Bouvier family should have a Bouvier, so he presented Caprice to Jacqueline Lee Bouvier, then living at 520 East 86th St. in New York City. Miss Bouvier, later the First Lady, was in 1942, perhaps, the first to enter a Bouvier at a Westminster show.

THE BREED'S STANDARDS

In purebred dogs, breeders, buyers and judges require a universally agreed upon standard for guidance in forming objectives and in making selections. In the United States the formulation of such a standard is the exclusive responsibility of the group designated by the American Kennel Club as the "parent club" for the subject breed. Almost invariably the designated club is the oldest continuously active group in the breed within the AKC framework.

In the preparation of a standard the AKC will offer guidance if it is requested, but the AKC philosophy is that a standard is strictly the prerogative and responsibility of those most familiar with and most active in a breed. The AKC does examine proposed standards for conflicts with AKC procedures and requirements, for errors in grammar and for understandability. A standard becomes operative when the AKC's directors formally approve it—after publication and opportunity for objections from interested parties. AKC show judges are instructed to use only an official standard as their criteria in making placements at shows.

The AKC does not permit illustrations, whether photographic or drawn, as official parts of a standard. An endlessly repeated comment is that no artist, never having seen an example of a subject breed, could draw a recognizable picture from a standard. Be that as it may, the official standard has been the only reasonable starting point for a serious student of any breed. Understanding gained from a study of the standard can be "fleshed out" by watching good breed examples at shows, by noting which types are winning—and by attempting to understand why. One caution: making evaluations from outside the ring is much more difficult for such dense-coated breeds as the Bouvier than it would be for smooth-coated breeds where outlines are clear and musculature and skeletal formation are often sufficiently visible to form bases for conclusions. Accurate evaluations can never be made from outside a show ring because they require a physical examination of the dog—touch and sight.

Most of the canine world's governing bodies have breed standards and procedures similar to the AKC's. With few exceptions they all operate from written but unillustrated standards. Because it is the only measuring stick of Bouvier quality at American dog shows the standard approved by the AKC on April 14, 1959 is here presented first. However Bouvier enthusiasts everywhere are extremely fortunate. In 1972 Belgium's and France's most successful breeders met and shaped explanations of and illustrations for the Franco-Belgium standard of 1961 which was recognized by the Federation Cynologique Internationale in 1965. For the late Florimond Verbanck participation was his last great contribution to Bouviers.

Now, for serious students of Bouviers there *is* a viable starting point. There are, however, variations between the Franco-Belgian standard and the AKC standard and it should be emphasized that the AKC document is the only one with official status in the United States.

Here is the current AKC standard for the Bouvier des Flandres, copyrighted in 1959 by the AKC and reproduced by kind permission:

Official AKC Standard for the Bouvier des Flandres

The Bouvier des Flandres is a rough-coated dog of notably rugged appearance as befitting an erstwhile cattle driver and farmers' helper of Flandres, and later an ambulance dog and messenger in World War I. He is a compact-bodied, powerfully built dog of upstanding carriage and alert, intelligent expression.

Head—The head is medium long, with the skull slightly longer than the muzzle. **Skull**—Almost flat on top, moderately wide between the ears, and sloping slightly toward the muzzle. The brow is noticeably arched over the eyes. The stop is shallow, and the under-eye fill-in good. **Ears**—Rough-coated, set high on the head and cropped to a triangular contour. They stand erect and are carried straight up. **Eyes**—Neither protruding nor sunken, the eyes are set a trifle obliquely in the skull and not too far apart. They are of medium size and very nearly oval. Preferred color, a dark nut-brown. Black eyes, although not considered faulty, are less desirable as contributing to a somber expression. Light-colored eyes, and staring or wild expression are faulty. **Muzzle**—Wide, deep and well filled out, the width narrowing gradually toward the tip of the nose. Cheeks are clean or flat-sided, the jaws powerful, and the lips dry and tight-fitting. A narrow muzzle, suggestive of weakness, is faulty. **Teeth**—Strong and white, with the canines set well apart, the teeth meet in a scissors bite. **Nose**—Black and well developed, the nostrils wide open. Across the top the contour is a trifle rounded as opposed to flat. Brown, pink and spotted noses are faulty.

Neck and Shoulders—The neck is well rounded, slightly arched, and carried almost upright, its thickness gradually increasing as it fits gracefully into the shoulders. Clean and dry at the throat. The shoulders are long and sloping.

Body—The brisket is deep, extending down at least to the point of the elbows, and of moderate width. **Back**—Short, strong and straight. **Loins**—Short, taut, and slightly arched in topline, while the rump is broad and square rather than sloping. Ribs are deep and well sprung. As advantageous for breeding purposes, slightly greater length of loin is permissible in bitches.

Tail—Set high, carried up, and docked to about 4 inches.

Legs and Feet—The leg bones, although only moderate in girth, are made to appear heavy because of their covering with thick, rough hair. **Forelegs**—Straight as viewed from the front or side, with elbows turned neither in nor out. **Hind Legs**—Hindquarters are firm and well muscled, with large, powerful hams. Legs are strong and sturdy, with hocks[1] well let down and wide apart. They are slightly angulated at stifle and hock joints. Viewed from the back, they are absolutely parallel.[2] **Feet**[3]—Round, compact, with toes arched and close. The nails are black, the pads thick and tough.

Coat—Rough, touseled and unkempt in appearance, the coat

1. It is important to understand that all normal dogs are digitigrade—meaning they walk on their toes. The "hock" is synonymous with "heel," meaning all bones below the hock are foot—not leg—bones. Ed.
2. Presumably this refers to an alert dog standing—but not in motion. Ed.
3. There is an error in terminology here. A rear foot, for example, starts at the hock and cannot possibly be "round." This section should be headed "paws" or "toes." Ed.

is capable of withstanding the hardest work in the most inclement weather. **Topcoat**—Harsh, rough and wiry, and so thick that when separated by the hand the skin is hardly visible. **Undercoat**—Fine and soft in texture, and thicker in winter. On the skull the hair is shorter and almost smooth. On the brows it is longer, thus forming eyebrows. Longer growth on muzzle and underjaw form mustache and beard. On the legs it is thick and rough, on the feet rather short. Soft, silky or woolly topcoats are faulty.

Color—From fawn to black, pepper and salt, gray and brindle. A white star on the chest is allowed. Chocolate brown with white spots is faulty.

Height—Dogs from 23½ to 27½ inches; bitches, a minimum of 22¾ inches.

SCALE OF POINTS[4]

Coat 20	Back, lion, brisket, belly 15
Head (eyes, ears, skull, foreface) 20	Feet and legs 10
Shoulders and style 10	Symmetry, size and character 15
Hindquarters (hams and legs) 10	TOTAL 100

Franco-Belgian Standard for the Bouvier des Flandres with Explanations by the Joint Commission

Translated by Miss Edmee F. Bowles

This exposition of the standard [European] for the Bouvier des Flandres is offered to make the physical qualities of the Bouvier des Flandres better understood. It was realized through the cooperative effort of the Club du Bouvier des Flandres pour la France and the Club National Belge du Bouvier des Flandres. Serving on the joint commission which prepared it were Messers Thorp, Malaquin, Martineau and Dr. Le Lann for France. Messers Chastel and Verbanck represented Belgium. The drawings are by M. Martineau, vice-president of the French club.

First published February 1, 1972 in a booklet as a joint venture, the text and accompanying illustrations are here reproduced by kind permission. (The standard appears in light face type. The joint commission's opinions are in italics.)

---

4. Scales of points are almost an anachronism in AKC standards. They are being phased out as standards are revised—perhaps because they invite subjective evaluations. Ed.

ORIGINS: The Bouvier des Flandres, as the name indicates originated in Flandres,—both French and Belgium as there are no boundaries separating these two countries.

It is difficult to ascertain exact origins. He was produced by circumstancial breeding. It is certain that shepherds and cattle herders of Flanders needed good dogs and selected locally for their moral and physical qualities rather than bred for a predetermined type. Present Bouviers have inherited these qualities.

The Bouvier is a result of crossings amongst hardy and rustic dogs. These selections for quality produced a uniformity which attracted serious dog breeders. In 1912 they established the first Bouvier standard.

To maintain and fix the type as to purity of the breed it was necessary to eliminate all faulty recessives, both moral and physical.

APTITUDES: In the beginning the Bouvier was used to herd cattle, for draught and butter churning. Modernization has changed farm equipment. Now the Bouvier is used as guard for home or farm, for defense or police work. His great physical and moral aptitudes, his excellent nose, initiative and intelligence make him an excellent tracker, and game keeper's aid.

Because of his strength, his mass, his gruff appearance, his intelligence, fidelity to his master and attachment to all that belongs to the family with whom he lives, the Bouvier is an extraordinary guard dog. He can defend with all his energy the house, factory, garden or car. Formidable guardian and protector of children and family he is, at the same time, their friend and playmate.

GENERAL CHARACTERISTICS: Cobby, short bodied and thickset on powerful and muscular limbs; gives the impression of power, without clumsiness as a whole. The fire in his eyes denotes intelligence, energy, and audacity. He is calm, rational and prudently bold.

He is cobby in length, as contrasted with lanky. He is a blocky dog without excessive weight which would cause him to lose his agility and mobility. A Bouvier too heavy would be unfit for his work; one too light would not be a Bouvier.

The moral qualities of the Bouvier are their heritage from ancestors selected for demanding work as herders.

The Bouvier is a well balanced dog, intelligent; i.e., he is safe. He is bold, prudent, obedient to his master and very courageous in his

Hagard expression

Whistle-like muzzle

Soft coat

Light eyes, bad coat

Ram's head, vanishing forehead

Forehead too long, head too light

Chiseled head

Bold expression

defense. He only bites when necessary. He is without meanness and he does not maul. His keen nose, well developed, makes him suitable as a war or police dog and also as a gamekeeper's helper.

THE HEAD: Massive, appearing more so because of his beard and mustache, it is well proportioned to his body and size. To the feel, it is finely chiseled.

The head by its shape and volume, is characteristic of the breed and has its own distinctive expression.

THE SKULL:—Well developed and flat, longer than its width. The top lines of the skull and muzzle are parallel. The proportions of the skull to the muzzle are 3 to 2.

These proportions 3 to 2 must be adhered to, as they are a characteristic of the breed. A rounded or narrow skull is a fault.

FRONTAL GROOVE:—Barely perceptible.

A deep frontal groove changes the expression of the head and gives it a common and undesirable expression.

STOP:—Barely percievable, more apparent than real because of the raised eyebrows.

The frontal-nasal angle should be between 140° and 150°.
If too open it gives a receding profile which is too sharp and a common undesirable expression.

MUZZLE:—Wide, powerful, bony, straight in upper profile, diminishing toward the nose but never pointed. The muzzle is shorter than the skull—in the proportion of 2 to 3 and the circumference just below the eyes is about equal to length of head.

The proportions 2 to 3 for length of skull to muzzle, must be adhered to. So must the cubic appearance. A pointed muzzle is a fault.

NOSE—This is the continuation of the muzzle; it is slightly convex at its extremity—must be well developed, rounded at its edges—and must always be black with well opened nostrils.

Whatever the color of the coat, the nose must always be black without any spots. They are an indication of degeneracy.

CHEEKS—Flat and dry.

Flat cheeks emphasize the fine chiseled look of the head. Rounded cheeks overly suggest the fullness of the Matin.

EARS—Cropped in a triangle, they are carried well up; attached high and very mobile. It is recommended that the size and shape should match the size of the head.

At attention the ears are well up. A dog which does not carry them up is often apt to be a shy dog, or out of condition.

The standard states cropping should be in proportion to the head. In general ⅔ should be left, but this is only our counsel.

Ears badly cropped, too long or too short, change the expression of the dog. The same applies to ears carried poorly.

EYES—Bold and energetic, neither prominent nor sunken. In shape slightly oval on a horizontal plane. The color should be as dark as possible in keeping with color of the coat. Light in color or haggard in expression should be severely faulted.

The color of the eye is very important, as the tint modifies the expression. Eyes should always be dark, whatever the color of the coat—and never lighter than a hazel nut.

A light eye gives a haggard expression—a sign of degeneration. Rounded, protruding eyes are a fault. The opening of the lids of the eyes should be slightly oval but not as much as the shape of an almond, nor almost oriental.

EYELIDS—Black without a trace of deficient pigmentation; No haw should be visible.

> *When the haw shows, it changes the expression. Drooping tissues often indicate a soft and lymphatic temperament. They are often the cause of accidents by irritation. They have a potential for infection from dust, pollen and grit.*

JAWS AND TEETH—Jaws should be powerful and of equal length; the teeth strong, white and healthy. The upper incisors must meet the lower ones like the blades of a scissors or fit like a pincers. [Even bite.]

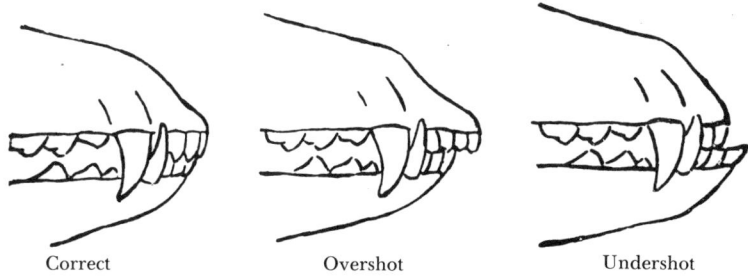

Correct   Overshot   Undershot

> *Jaws should be of equal length. If the upper jaw is longer the dog is overshot. If the lower is longer the dog is undershot. Either is a serious and degenerate fault which must be dealt with severely. In a scissors bite the inside of the upper incisors slide over the lower incisors making a minimal contact. Absence of contact here would be defined as overshot. The opposite constitutes an overshot bite. A pincer bite indicates a perfect set of jaws.*
>
> *The number of teeth is 42. Those with brownish marks, pitted or with enamel otherwise marred indicate previous decalcification. These esthetic faults should be evaluated accordingly. Some dogs have teeth covered with tartar which should be scaled off. Care should be taken to avoid scratching the enamel. With age teeth can turn yellow. This is only a sign of age and not a genetic consideration.*

NECK—The neck should be free—strong-muscled and widening into the shoulders. Its length should be slightly less than that of the head. The nape should be powerful and slightly arched. There should be no dewlap.

> *The power of a Bouvier's attack lies not only in the spring of his quarters—but in the power of his neck and jaws. The neck therefore must be powerful without being sunk into the shoulders. The head must be joined to the trunk by a continuous line*

without a sharp angle to the shoulders. The nape should be slightly arched. A good set of the neck is characteristic of a well-bred animal. A cylindrical neck, round like a stove pipe, is faulty.

WITHERS—Slightly prominent.

The withers are the points of the shoulder blades. These bony points are used to measure the height of the dog. The height at the withers is determined by dropping a perpendicular line to the floor, passing at the point of the elbow. It is indicated in centimeters.[1]

GUIDE TO TERMINOLOGY OF MEASUREMENTS

A Height measured from ground to top of withers. B Height of croup. C Thoractic perimeter (not a straight line). D Length of the torso. E Length of the head. F Length of the cranium. G Length of the muzzle. H Width of the head.

1. In almost all of the world except North America.

BODY OR TRUNK—Powerful, cobby and short. The length of the point of the shoulder to ischium should be about equal to the height at the withers. The ischium is the rear point of the rump. The chest should reach to level of elbows, and never be cylindrical, though the ribs are well sprung. The depth, i.e., the distance between the sternum and the last rib must be great—about $7/10$ths of the height at the withers.

The length of the trunk (or torso) is measured between two bony points which do not vary—from the points of the shoulder to the ischium.

RIBS—The first ribs are slightly curved; the others are well sprung and well inclined to the rear giving the desired depth of the chest. Flat ribs must be greatly penalized.

The Bouvier, being a powerful dog, must have bulk. This means a well developed thoracic cage with a deep, almost barrel-like chest.

Flat or ogival ribs narrow the chest by reducing its volume [including heart and lung room]. The result is a look opposite to barrel-like. [Ribs pivot inward and outward to some degree with inhalation and exhalation—so there is no arc which can be mathematically expressed.]

The depth of the chest should be such that the low point of the sternum reaches the level of the elbows. The chest should be of sufficient that the dog does not appear out at the elbows.

FLANK—The flank between the last rib and the haunch must be very short, especially in males. There is very little tuck up.

Seen from the side the sternum with the belly makes a slight curve rising into the line of the flank. The flank must be short, the belly full. The dog that shows much daylight under him like a coursing hound must be penalized.

BACK—Short, wide, muscled and firm—showing no weakness but remaining flexible.

It is essential that a Bouvier be cobby. This necessitates a short, powerful and firm back. A swayed or roached back indicates a malformation of the spine and a genetic defect.

LOIN—Short, wide and well muscled—must remain flexible but without any weakness.

This description is very clear and needs no explanation.

CROUP OR RUMP—Must follow as closely as possible the horizontal line of the back and follow [merge] smoothly into the curve of the rump. It should be wide without excess in the male, more developed [wider] in the female. A descending [steeply tilted] croup is a serious fault.

Tilted croup; hindquarters underslung; weak and frail legs; poor set of neck.

Light, lacks chest; hindquarters too long; flat thighs.

Light, poor tail set.

Swaybacked and barrel-chested.

Too long; lacks chest; swayback; neck like the flue of a stove.

Swaybacked; tilted croup; too much daylight under belly; lightly built.

BOUVIER BODY CONFORMATION

Admirable cobbiness.

Standing under, descending croup.

Powerful, cobby and short.

A descending or tilted croup, one that is significantly more than the 40° illustrated in the accompanying drawing [McDowell Lyon and some other authorities have felt it should be nearer to a 30° tilt], is due to an excessive tilt of the pelvis and a grave fault.

Indeed, if the pelvis is too inclined the rear legs [and support] are too much under the body. This restricts the dog's reach in moving. With the paws placed too far forward the thrust from the rear tends to elevate the body. The up and down motion wastes energy without productivity in forward progress. The gait is fatiguing and defective. A descending croup results from either an insufficiency of the muscles in that region or a genetically caused excessive slope of the pelvic bones with an accompanying low set tail.

A croup like a mule's with a sharp spine and a lateral falling away is also a fault. A happily carried tail should not be at a right angle to the spine — but rather a continuation of the spine.

Correct proportions and angulation of the Bouvier des Flandres.

FRONT ASSEMBLY

FOREQUARTERS—The forequarters should have a strong bony structure, well muscled and perfectly straight.

Fiddle front.　　　　　　　Correct　　　　　　　Pigeon toed.
(Toes turn out.)　　　　　　　　　　　　　　　(Toes turn in.)

SHOULDERS AND FOREARMS—The shoulders are relatively long, well muscled, not loaded and moderately oblique. The humerus and shoulder blades are almost the same length.

> *The shoulders must be sufficiently oblique to permit free action of the elbows. The Bouvier is a trotter, the angle of the shoulder blade with horizontal should be 58°. An angle too open would mean too straight a shoulder and would hamper forward thrust.*

ELBOWS—Close to the body and parallel. Elbows out or too close are faults. In action they must remain parallel to median line of the body.

> *If the elbows are out and are not on a parallel plane of the median line of the body weight then sways in an oblique line.*

FOREARMS—seen from profile or front they remain straight, parallel to each other and perpendicular to ground. They should be well muscled and of powerful bony structure.

> *The length of the forearm should be about ⅓ of the height at withers. Forearms that are concave or convex are a sign of rickets.*

CARPAL (KNEE)—In plumb with the forearms, except for the accessory carpal at the back. Strong and heavy bone.

> *The carpal represents the wrist, which articulates the junction of the forarm with the hand, or front foot.*

METACARPALS—of strong bony structure, very slightly inclined forward.

Metacarpus (pastern) too upright. Causes knee (arrow) to bulge.

Correct

Pastern too long. Paws too far forward.

If the metacarpals, or pasterns, are inclined too far forward it gives the appearance of leaning on the wrists; if too straight they cause a bulge at the carpals and curtail the suppleness of gait.

FRONT PAWS—short, round and compact. The toes should be close and well arched. Nails—strong and black. Thick and hard soles.

Hare foot. Too long.

Correct paw for a Bouvier.

Flat and splay-footed.

Paws that are flat and open toed are a fault.

POSTERIOR MEMBERS [rear legs]—Powerful and pronounced musculature is demanded. Rear legs must move in the same plane as the anterior members [front legs].

THIGHS—Wide and well muscled. The direction will be parallel to the median plane of the body. The femurs will be neither too straight nor too inclined. The buttock will be well let down with good, firm breeches. The kneecap, or patella, is situated on an imaginary line from the iliac crest to the ground.

The rump should be thick—but not like a leg of mutton. A narrow and flat rump is a fault. The slope of the femur should be about 70° to the horizontal [when the metacarpals are perpendicular to the ground].

LEGS—Moderately long, neither too straight nor too inclined.

The average inclination of the tibia should be about 60° [when the metacarpals are perpendicular to the ground] to the horizontal and the dog is posed in a "stand, stay" position. As seen from behind (see accompanying illustrations) to the tip of the hock [heel] is on a line from the ischium tip to and perpendicular to the ground when the vertebral colums is horizontal.

HOCKS—Rather close to the ground, broad, well muscled and stretched. Seen from back they will be straight and parallel in the "stand" position. In action they remain parallel.[2]

Seen from behind, the hocks, whether in stand or action, remain parallel—otherwise the dog is close or out.

METATARSI—Strong and dry, rather cylindrical; perpendicular to the ground when in position "stand". No dewclaws.

The metatarsi, or shanks, with the tarsus form the posterior shank. In "stand, stay," as seen from profile, they must be perpendicular to the ground. The correct angulation of croup, buttock, leg and shank, makes for a good rear.

POSTERIOR PAWS—Round, strong, toes close and arched. Strong, black nails and thick, hard soles.

The posterior paws must be free from dewclaws—and surely not double ones—which could only result from a random, distant and unwelcome recessive trait. Dewclaws are prone to being torn off in accidents

---

2. This requirement is in absolute opposition to a preponderance of the findings resulting from scientific investigations. It is also in direct disagreement with virtually every authority on animal locomotion. Ed.

This dog's support at rest is misplaced. The center of his pads should be directly under the points of his pelvis (bone underlying the rump or croup). His metacarpi, those bones of the foot below the hock, should be on an axis with these points. His support should be A - B, not c - d. While his metacarpi are parallel as viewed from the rear they are too close. Lines of force will tend to converge when in motion and gaining speed, but this dog at rest has precarious balance because of his narrow base. Also, he consumes extra energy since he must make muscular compensations for his structural defect. whether in motion or standing

Out at hocks. Line of support not straight requiring more muscular effort and energy just to stand up.

Correct rear support.

Hocks turned in. Cow hocked. Line of support not straight requiring extra energy just to stand.

THE BOUVIER'S DRIVING GEAR

COAT—The coat is very full. The top coat plus the dense undercoat make a perfect wrap adapted to the abrupt climatic changes characteristic of the breed's country of origin.

The Bouvier is equipped with a true mantle composed of an outer coat which sheds rain and a dense undercoat which is waterproof. This equips him to be truly resistant to inclemencies and it assures his rusticity.

COLORS—The coat of the Bouvier des Flandres is generally fawn or grey, often brindle or dark grey. Black is also allowed but is not to be favored. Light-colored coats and washed out colors are not desirable.

The standard does not allow white, yellow or salt and pepper. These are faults. Dark brindle is the ideal color. At the moment many Bouvier breedings show tendencies toward ever lighter colors on the washed out side. These are throwbacks to ancient ancestors. We have to fight this and select very dark brindles for breeding.

COAT—It must be rough to the touch, harsh and dry—neither too long nor too short (about 2½ inches), slightly tousled without ever being woolly or curly.

On the head the coat is shorter and almost shaved on the outside of the ear, but the inside is protected by fairly long hair. On the top of the back the coat is harsh or dry; it becomes shorter on the lower legs, while still harsh. A flat coat is to be avoided since it indicates a lack of undercoat.

One of the characteristics of the breed is the coat which, while harsh to the touch all over the dog, should be dry and dull, neither too long nor too short (about 2½ inches). It should be slightly tousled without being flat or curly. It must not be woolly in spite of the dense, waterproof undercoat. Many paradoxes are hard to reconcile.

To maintain some sense of balance in these seeming conflicts the breeder will need constant adjustments. He will have to watch so the coat does not become too long and thereby too soft; or too short thereby too smooth and too close. He must obtain a dog with a harsh and slightly tousled coat as the standard requires.

UNDERCOAT—A wadding made of fine and close hairs grows under the outercoat and forms with it to provide a waterproof mantle.

The undercoat of the Bouvier can be compared to the lining of a raincoat which protects him from the weather. This is a characteristic of the breed which permits him to resist the tough climatic

Too harsh; no undercoat.

Briard-type coat. Flat and too long.

Coat wooly and too long.

Washed out color.

Coat too short and flat.

Coat rough to the touch.

Dry coat.

A quality coat.

Slightly tousled coat.

A quality coat.

changes of his native land and it is conducive to his hardiness. The absence of undercoat is therefore a fault. It is also displeasing because the overall result is a flat and unattractive overall appearance of the coat.

MUSTACHE AND BEARD—Fully dry, shorter and harsher on top of muzzle. The upper lip has a mustache and the chin has a full, harsh beard which gives the gruff expression so characteristic of the breed.

The mustache and beard form the furnishings of the head giving to the Bouvier that gruff expression so characteristic of the breed.

EYEBROWS—These are made of upstanding hair which accentuate the arch of the eyebrows without ever hiding the eyes.

At the level of the stop there is a lock of hair bent forward—but without falling on the muzzle. This would give the appearance of a Briard and be an important fault in a Bouvier.

SKIN—Firm, without excessive laxity; visible mucous membranes are always very dark.

The skin of the Bouvier should neither be too tight nor too loose. The pigmentation of the lips should always be very dark. Pink exterior lips is a sign of loss of pigmentation—and a fault.

EXTERNAL SEXUAL ORGANS—well developed. In the male the testicles must be in place.

In the males, monorchid or bilateral cryptorchidism is disqualifying.

HEIGHT—Height at the withers for males is $24\frac{3}{8}$ to $26\frac{3}{4}$ inches. Females $23\frac{1}{4}$ to $24\frac{5}{8}$ inches. In each sex the average is between these limits, i.e., $25\frac{1}{2}$ for males and $24\frac{1}{2}$ for females.

WEIGHT—Approximately 77 to 88 pounds for males; 60 to 77 pounds for females.

GAIT: The Bouvier des Flandres as a whole must be harmoniously proportioned to permit a gait free, proud and bold. The walk and trot are habitual gaits though ambling and pacing are also employed.

The gait of the Bouvier is very characteristic; it is that of a determined and bold dog, i.e. free and harmonious. It shows the functional conformation of the dog but also his temperament and is thus, very important. The dog which shows himself shyly, with stilted movement, head and ears low, and tail down surely is shy and should be eliminated from a breeding program in spite of good conformation.

The gait of the Bouvier is that of a trotter. This gait is conditioned by his conformation and the articular angles of his limbs which have to move in parallel planes and perpendicular to the ground.[3] *Bad stance both front and rear, either too out or too close, are the consequences of poor conformation. Such faults result in poor gait and are therefore serious.*

GRAVE FAULTS

CONFORMATION: Long in body.
EYES: Light.
EARS: Not erect.
BITE: Overshot or undershot.
RIBS: Flat, too long or overly rounded and short.
CROUP: Descending [overtilted].
COAT: Washed out colors.
HAIR: Soft, woolly, silky, too long or too short.

SERIOUS FAULTS

BUILD: Sway back.
COAT: Lack of undercoat.
HAIR: White star on chest allowed but not desireable.

DISQUALIFYING FAULTS

EYES: Wall eyed, haggard expression.
NOSE: Spotted or butterfly.
COAT: Chocolate brown—too much white.
SEXUAL ORGANS: Monorchid or bilateral cryptorchid.

The characteristics of the Bouvier des Flandres were first defined by a standard in 1912. This standard was followed by two distinct standards, one by the French Bouvier breeders, the other by the Belgium National Club of the Bouvier des Flandres.

The Club of the Bouvier des Flandres and other friends of the Bouvier in France and the Club National Belge du Bouvier des Flandres joined in 1961 to shape and jointly adopt a single standard. This is the standard here given. It was accepted by the Federation Cynologique International in 1965.

---

3. See footnote, page 161.

BREEDING BOUVIERS, WHELPING AND RAISING THE LITTER
BY MARION HUBBARD

THE great hope of a conscientious breeder is that he or she will create something better of its kind than the world has ever known before. Without that motivation—and relative possibilities of its realization—there can be no reason for breeding.

The usual reasons are all invalid in the eyes of objective breeders. Here are some of them:

1. "Queenie needs sexual experience. Let her have some fun." (She'll hardly know what she has been missing until after she has experienced it.) "Every bitch should have one litter." (A pure and simple old wives' tale.)

2. "Breed Queenie and make money on the puppies." (Breeding for quality is almost always more loss than profit. And, somehow, only inferior puppies seem to result from profit breeding. Dogs are social creatures that require personal attention. They are not commodities.)

3. "I love my Queenie and I want one of her puppies." (This is the way most breeders start—and the way they get lost in a maze of undefined and unknown genetic characteristics. Frustrated, most drop out before they can make any progress. Love any dog you wish, but breed from quality with predictable genetic possibilities.)

4. "Queenie got caught so we might as well let her have the puppies." (Queenie knows and cares less about mate selection than the most careless and uninformed breeder. Get Queenie to a vet for "morning after" shots.)

5. "The experience of having Queenie's puppies born and raised in the house will be good for the children—and something of a cop-out for me in conveying sex education to my kids." (The same advantages accrue when having a quality-bred litter.)

6. "This dog game can't be so complicated that a bright and successful person like me can't figure it out in a hurry and move right to the top. Besides, I know a good dog when I'm looking at it." (Another "three month" or even "three year expert" in the making. Learn first. Pick the brains of all who might be able to help. Attend shows just to study the dogs. Read, not just about one breed of dog but about all of them. And know this. No one—but no one—can judge dogs just by looking at them. Certainly it would be impossible to do so in a dense coated breed like Bouviers. Judging must also be done with knowledgeable hands—and often a little heart.)

7. This is the predictable switch on numbers one, two and three. "Prince is lonely—in fact very sexy. I'll make him happy by getting him a female to breed with." (Bitches are breedable about ten days a year. What's Prince going to do the other 355 days after you have gotten him stirred up by letting him find out what he has been missing? If you have a male worth breeding from, owners of good bitches will come looking for him. If Prince is all that lonely and needs a pet of his own get him a cat or a turtle.)

If you are going to breed dogs you might as well do what you can to insure the venture's success. Be hard-headed and deliberate. You cannot create better than the best unless you start with the best. Study the strengths and weaknesses of the various leading kennels. Remember that genetic characteristics are not all visible. Get a known genetic inventory. Make sure your foundation stock comes from line bred winners. Don't get involved with scrambled genetics. You could spend many years and dollars getting things unscrambled.

If you feel you are not up to studying the complexities for yourself go to two or three breeders of winning stock. Make allowances because each of them will be oversold on his own dogs. At this point you will be picking a breeder as well as a puppy. Select well. The right breeder can become a most helpful mentor for you.

Note this well. The right time to buy a puppy is *not* on the day you decide to buy a puppy. *The right time to buy a puppy is on the day the right puppy becomes available to you.*

The best stock is often reserved months before the mating is made. The best stock is worth waiting for.

If you are ever going to spend money on a dog do it when you are buying your foundation bitch. That first bitch's influence will be evident in your kennel as long as you are breeding from her descendents.

One thing more: remember that temperament is the one most important characteristic in any dog. You can live with almost anything except a bad temperament. It is bad enough living with a bad temperament—breeding from it should be a punishable offense.

A knowledgeable veterinarian is important. Many well-recommended veterinarians don't like Bouviers. Ask breeders in your area for the names of good men. Find one who is interested in breeding purebred dogs in general—one who won't suggest spaying your valuable bitch at the first sign of internal problems after she has had a litter, or one who feels a certain animosity towards you because you are in a breed which requires cosmetic surgery.

You must have rapport with your vet so that when you come to him with questions on breeding your bitch or raising your litter, he will spend the time and the effort necessary to consider your specialized problems. Veterinarians with little experience in pure-bred dogs or too busy a practice will prove unworthwhile. Personal interest goes a long way toward making the difference between average medical advice and quality care.

Beware of the vet who always has an answer—even on such subjects as genetics and nutrition on which he has probably had no formal training. When you find a vet who can say: "I don't know." that is a very good indicator.

The brood bitch candidate should be in good health and free of parasites. Don't just worm your bitch as she is coming in season and feel that she is then in good health. It is necessary to consider your dog's health long in advance of the season in which you plan to breed her. Have her in moderate weight, worm-free at least six months prior to breeding and checked regularly. Keep her (distemper, hepatitis, leptospirosis) shots up to date. Our dogs have boosters every six months. Do not breed your bitch if she has skin problems. Eighteen months of age is as young as you should want to breed a bitch. Judge by age, not the number of seasons.

The selection of the stud dog should have the same deliberate judgement as was given to the bitch's acquisition. Most of the same criteria pertain. Again you won't want scrambled genetics, not, at least, until after you've acquired considerable breeding experience.

If you are inexperienced you had better trust the public record rather than your own judgement. Insist that the sire be a winner of some note or, even better, a producer of notable winners.

Don't be dazzled by a pedigree full of champions. In itself the title (except under the Federation Cynologique Internationale) can have a limited meaning. "Bests of breeds" in a minority breed such as Bouviers could mean the dog has had only himself to defeat. Champions have been made in many breeds, including Bouviers, by competing only against kennelmates—or even littermates. The table of "Bouviers defeated" has more meaning. So do group placements. The "Bouviers defeated" table does, however, require some explanation. Say there are enough bitches showing in the classes to comprise a "major" toward a championship—but only one dog in the classes. That dog becomes "winners dog" almost automatically. He has an opportunity to also gain a major of the same number of points if he defeats the "winners bitch" for "best of winners." It is the custom of some judges to spread the points around. It doesn't take anything really significant away from the bitch but it gives treasured credit to the dog. It has also made it easier for the dog to become a champion. *Examine the quality of a prospective stud's victories.*

Ask the owners of the stud candidates if you can go over them. Train your hands as well as your eyes. The owners will be glad to point out the dogs' best qualities. It's up to you (or someone helping you) to determine the faults.

It would be helpful to have a qualified person go over your bitch and fault her. Be objective! Try to select a mate that will compliment her and perhaps help her weaker points.

Don't just breed to a dog who lives in the next town or the current most-winning dog. Raising a good litter of puppies is just as costly as raising a poor litter—and the time involved can seem endless. You should make every effort to improve each new generation.

In considering a stud dog it would be wise to look at his get. Ask for a copy of his pedigree. Know whether you would be line breeding or out-crossing. When evaluating a stud's get give weight to the qualities of the bitch that whelped his puppies. What did she add, or subtract, from the litter's quality? Do puppies or young adults sired by the stud have the same faults or weak points you see in your own bitch? If so, seek another male.

A list of some of the more common failings in Bouviers follows, not necessarily in order of seriousness: Weak hindquarters, long backs, light eyes, straight shoulders, no spring of ribs, too much white on the chest, lack of furnishings and flat coat, undershot and overshot bites, too much undercoat in comparison to top coat, no neck, oversized and undersized dogs, dogs with small heads in proportion to their bodies or are otherwise out of balance, loosely-knit dogs that shamble, clumsy, thick-set dogs that are coarse and without grace and style.

After you've selected the stud, thoroughly discuss your agreement with his owner. Then reduce the agreement to a written and signed contract with copies for each. Neither the courts nor the AKC will recognize anything except a written contract. And, there *are* many misunderstandings and disagreements in such relationships.

It is the stud owner's responsibility to handle the actual mating. You may be asked to steady your bitch or hold her head but the owner of the male conducts the affair.

If the stud is inexperienced you probably shouldn't have considered him and certainly not for a maiden bitch. But if you've committed yourself it is reasonable to ask his owner to have the dog's sperm checked for count and motility. You won't want to wait a month or more watching for signs of pregnancy, or to miss a breeding season, because the stud lacks sufficient of what is vital. The same holds for aging studs. This practice has another benefit. Ejaculate stored in a male's body diminishes with time. That's one reason why second or third day repeats of matings are common practice. Another is to insure that viable sperm will be available when actual ovulation takes place.

The *average* term for a canine pregnancy is 63 days. Your pre-natal care of the puppies begins almost at once. Keep your bitch on a normal diet for the first month even though she may be asking for more food. *Do not fatten her up.* Supplement her feedings with a good pre-natal vitamin as Natabec (Park-Davis) daily during pregnancy. Extra protein food is recommended. I use a half-ounce of liver daily. At about a month into gestation your bitch will lose interest in food for several days. This is a good indication that she is in whelp. Her appetite will come back quickly and *do* feed her well at this time.

You may find you want to put her on three meals daily to give her sufficient food. As the whelps grow it will become increasingly difficult for her to consume sufficient food in two large meals. Ask your veterinarian about proper quantities for your bitch. Trotting exercise is very good for your pregnant Bouvier. Cut or hand strip the coat on your bitch two to three weeks prior to whelping. Remove the coat from around her teats and cut it very short in the vaginal area.

Organize your whelping room well in advance of the event. A good quiet room with outside access is best. Remember that your bitch will want to go outside to relieve herself frequently and that you won't want her tracking through the house, at least for the first few days after whelping. Try to select quarters, in any case, where neighborhood children will not be walking through and where you can maintain an even temperature. If the dam and her puppies seem in good condition I do not maintain too warm a room. I prefer $60°-65°$ Do not permit young children to approach closely or to handle the whelps. Measles can be a disaster for your puppies. Besides, intruders worry a bitch and she might react forcefully.

The whelping box should be constructed several weeks before the puppies arrive so your bitch can become accustomed to her new quarters. It may be built of $\frac{3}{4}''$ plywood or 1 x 8 inch stock. The latter is easier to saw with simple tools but not as durable. Our boxes are 4 x 8 feet. This allows the bitch adequate room to move about. And, as the puppies develop, they will crawl away from the dam to relieve themselves. Dogs are naturally clean. If the puppies are kept clean and have sufficient space they will quickly learn to move away from their living quarters before defecating.

The box should have a "pig rail" about four to five inches above the floor. This keeps the bitch from getting flush against the sides and allows space for the puppies to crawl behind the bitch without becoming stuck or smothered against the sides of the box. A two inch by four inch board turned on edge and bolted to the sides and ends of the box serves well.

A plastic covered foam mattress, one to two inches thick (made by you) makes a good floor. The resilient surface acts to protect the puppies if the dam accidentally steps on them; it is more comfortable for your bitch; it is easily wiped clean. We cover the mattress with toweling sewn to a five foot by 10 foot size. The rough surface is absorbent and provides good footing for the whelps. The covers are changed as necessary to keep the box clean.

The whelping box should have a door cut into its side just above the pig rail. This should be hinged and have slide bolt fasteners at the top. The door will permit the dam to come and go during the first weeks. Later, when the puppies are about three weeks old, you can close the door to keep them from climbing out. By that time the dam will be with the pups only to wash them and nurse them.

The materials and equipment needed for normal puppy whelping are minimal. Have on hand paper toweling, newspaper for the box prior to and during whelping (put the mattress into the box *after* whelping), a large plastic trash can with liners, a wicker basket in which to place the whelps after birth so that the dam won't step on them while whelping and cleaning her next puppy and a heat lamp to keep the newborn whelps warm. Do not place the lamp close enough to the newborn puppies to burn their skin. Be prepared with towels you won't mind staining. Use these to rub the whelps dry. A blunt-nose scissors for trimming umbilical cords may be necessary. Use a disinfectant, such as Lysol, to wipe the mattress clean. A rectal thermometer can be helpful, as will a scale, notebook and clock if you are keeping records. Esbilac and premature baby bottles should also be available for supplemental feeding.

We never let our bitches whelp unattended, and we have never found the temperature drop suggested by all the books written on whelping to be very relevant. Some bitches' temperatures do drop several days prior to whelping but we have had others go all day with a normal temperature and then late in the evening start labor. Before we could check her temperature the first puppy would arrive.

During whelping try to keep the bitch as clean as possible. Some try to eat the afterbirth. We allow the dam to eat several if she desires, but dispose of the majority. *Do* keep count of the afterbirths—all should be expelled.

It is most important that the sac be broken and the puppy's mouth lifted clear of membranes and fluids with breathing started as soon as possible. Do not allow the dam to drag the whelp about by the umbilical cord. If necessary, press the remaining blood down the cord toward the whelp. Sever the cord by grasping it firmly between thumb and forefinger of one hand about an inch from the navel. With your other hand take a similar hold another inch away from the pup. Pull with the hand furthest away until the cord breaks. Do not pull the cord away in such a manner that you put pressure on the navel. That will cause an umbilical hernia. Wipe each pup briskly with a towel simulating the mother's licking them to stimulate their systems.

You may want to offer your bitch some milk and brandy during a long whelping. Sponge off and dry the dam's hindquarters after she is finished.

After your bitch is through whelping, it is necessary to take her to the veterinarian for a pituitrin shot, anti-biotics, and to be checked for possible retention of afterbirths or unborn whelps. If you have doubts about her puppies put them in a wicker wash basket lined with toweling. Cover them well and take them along. Pups with birth defects such as cleft palates, open abdomens, and crooked jaws can be dealt with by the vet if you haven't the moxie to do it yourself. Pups should have their dewclaws removed and their tails docked at three to five days of age. I advise making arrangements with the vet for these services before the actual whelping. You won't have time to shop for a vet later. Go by appointment. You won't be sitting with your pups in a waiting-room full of sick dogs.

Following whelping, your bitch will probably only want chicken broth, bouillon, or milk. Her water bowl should be kept full at all times. A liquid or semi-soft diet for 48 hours following whelping is a good idea. Protein makes milk; maintain a high protein diet with things like eggs, cheese, and meat. Continue the vitamins. You may find that it is necessary to feed the dam every 4–5 hours, depending on the size of the litter and her physical condition. Do not supplement feed the whelps for the first 48 hours unless necessary. The bitch's milk during the first hours passes temporary immunity to the pups for all those diseases to which the bitch has a resistance. Esbilac was mentioned earlier as advisable to have on hand. This commercial product is a synthetic bitch's milk. It is a fine supplement for the nursing dam and it might be needed at any time to help out the weaker puppies—or all of them if the bitch's milk fails. We like to bottle feed the puppies once daily. We use Esbilac and doll bottles but there is another way with a catheter tube your vet can demonstrate for you. The puppies are more readily weaned as a result of hand feeding and they are handled daily which is very important to their emotional development.

At about three weeks of age start training the puppies to eat from a dish. A convenient and easily digested mixture is a combination of Esbilac and prescription ID diet purchased from your vet. The ID diet may be run through a blender—thinned out with water or Esbilac. Use just a small quantity of the canned food to start. We train each puppy to lap—either on the floor or in our laps. This keeps their coats from becoming clogged with sticky food. As the puppies become more proficient at eating put them all on the floor to eat from a shallow baking pan outside the whelping box. Raise the pan height by using short pieces of two by four laid on their edges. A combination of wash cloth and dam helps clean them up following the meal. Our puppies are raised on Esbilac and the ID diet to between five and six weeks of age. Then they are gradually switched to a quality dry meal, and powdered skim milk and beef. Do not change the puppies' diet abruptly or diarrhea will result. Use a minimum of powdered vitamins in the food. We like Prenatal Theralin.

Between three and four weeks of age the puppies will start outgrowing the whelping box. Either double the size of their living quarters with one area for activity and one for sleep, or move them to a larger facility. Our pups are put in a whelping room with a concrete floor and outside door. They can come and go as soon as they can walk. A raised platform covered with toweling serves as a bed. Be careful not to keep pups on a slippery floor as paw and hip problems may result.

The following schedule is very convenient for Bouvier puppy care.

3–5 days:	Tails docked, dewclaws removed.
3 weeks;	Worm with piperazine adipate.
3–4 weeks:	Wean puppies away from dam.
5 weeks:	Worm again.
6 weeks:	First DHL vaccine shot.
7 weeks:	Ears cropped.
8 weeks:	Sutures out.
9 weeks:	Second DHL shot and either worm again or check stools.
12 weeks to 3 months:	Third DHL shot.

The Bouvier is basically a guard dog and some puppies exhibit guarding tendencies earlier than others. Do start giving the puppies a great deal of attention from three weeks on. Play with them, handle them, talk to them. A radio in the whelping room with talk shows on is one good method of helping to socialize them. They should be encouraged to go outside as soon as they have their feet under them. If the weather isn't severe let them out, rain or shine. By the time the puppies have a second DHL shot, we like to have our friends drop by to play with them and expose the litter to new faces and new situations. Do not keep them cloistered away.

You should consider the problem of ear-cropping before your bitch whelps. Start looking for a veterinarian who will crop the puppies' ears. Ask Bouvier breeders who live near you for names of competent men. It is worth driving some distance if you feel that you will have better ear crops. Perhaps your own vet is willing to try. If so, you must be prepared to instruct him as to shape and method. If you use someone who comes well-recommended, look at the ears on puppies or adults he has done. Do compare these with the shape on the Belgian imports—always excellent. The ear should be triangular and not too tall. *Be sure to stipulate no bell shape.* The length of the ear is measured to the outer corner of the eye, when cropping a young puppy. The ears should be sutured, and allowed to hang free. They heal more rapidly this way and it is easier to get them to stand erect later. Do not tape them down over the skull. This method puts a crease in the cartilage which is very difficult to overcome later on. The sutures are removed a week after the operation. The ears should be allowed to heal completely before any taping is considered. Hydrogen peroxide, applied twice daily, is excellent to promote healing. After the ears are healed massage helps a great deal to encourage the ears to stand. So does an exercise manipulating the ears backward and forward on the head so the puppy gains control of those ear muscles which pull the ears backward and parallel with the neck.

Masking tape works very well if you need to tape the ears in an upright position. Buy the ¾" width. It adheres well to the ears and comes off readily. If you have a particularly difficult set of ears with heavy cartilage ask your veterinarian for some ether to soften the adhesive on cloth tape and then adhere this to the ears.

The coat should be kept short on the ears and skull if you are taping ears. The coat should be cut short on the ears in any case as it makes it easier for the ears to assume correct carriage without additional weight. As the permanent teeth come in, you will notice that the ears tend to drop. This situation is only temporary and will correct itself.

At about three months of age, you will begin to see major changes in your puppies. If you have been undecided about which puppies to keep it is wise to wait until after these changes to make final decisions. You may want to ask another breeder his opinion. Or ask a professional handler or judge who knows working dogs.

GROOMING YOUR BOUVIER
BY LIL MEES

THE Bouvier's double coat enables him to adapt to the most drastic types of weather, and one finds that he can easily adapt to all climates. Wet, cold, foggy weather so typical of his homeland is no hardship for our friend; neither is snow nor hot sun. However long exposures to the sun will brown and tinge the coat. The orangeness or brownness one sometimes sees in the beard is not from sunburn but is usually from food and water staining.

Shedding by Bouviers can be kept minimal. A stiff brushing once or twice a week, getting vigorously down into the dead hairs will forestall most of the noticeable shedding.

For grooming use a table the dog can easily jump up on and one that will be easy for you to work around. Bouviers normally enjoy the attention of grooming, brushing, combing and trimming.

It is not necessary to bathe a Bouvier often—only when he becomes "dirty" to the touch. His rough, tousled coat tends to repell water, dirt and grime.

Most owners find their Bouviers enjoy a bath occasionally. In the summer a good rinsing down with the hose and a good pet shampoo will keep your Bouvier clean and sweet-smelling. Most Bouviers enjoy water and are excellent swimmers.

For more than mere maintainence grooming an owner should go

Bouvier grooming is a step by step procedure when Lil Mees' instructions are followed in conjunction with her outline drawing, above.

over his dog in the manner described in the remainder of this chapter at least once every four weeks.

Basic grooming requires that once a week you brush your dog with a slicker brush and comb out with a coarse comb. Cut his nails. Clean his teeth with a tooth scaler followed by scrubbing with baking soda on a damp wash cloth or toothbrush: and clean his *outer* ears thoroughly by rubbing them with a cotton ball dampened in alcohol. To trim, start out with a completely brushed and combed dog.

1. Trim hair on the ears very short on the outside and down to the leather on the amputated part. This may be done with a scissors or a #1 blade on electric clippers. With tweezers pull out all the hair on the

A slicker brush is used to unsnarl the facial furnishings. Care should be taken not to scratch the ears or eyes. Grooming photos by Howard Kling.

inside of the ear, especially the long hairs in the canal. Trim close with the scissors at the lower part of the ear just above the jawbone.

2. Cut the hair on top of the skull from the occiput to the eyebrows and down to the temples to a length of about one-half inch. This can be done with a thinning scissors or a #7 blade.

3. Eyebrows should be trimmed back to about one inch long with thinning scissors and a trimming knife. Avoid a sharp effect. Hair between the eyes should not be removed or trimmed across (as with a terrier). Allow it to come down over the muzzle, trimming at the nostrils.

In trimming hair along the edges of the ears care must be taken not to nip the ear. Use a strong light and rest fidgety dogs.

Thinning shears are used to shorten the hair over the eyes. This permits the Bouvier to see better and his expression to be seen better. Some groomers prefer to leave this hair a bit longer than is illustrated. Eyebrows can be hand plucked but the difference gained in appearance isn't worth the discomfort to the dog.

4. Brush and comb the beard thoroughly, trimming excessive length only. With a trimming knife thin out cheek hairs. Avoid a 'chipmunk' look, blending and working the cheek hairs into a heavy beard.

5. Beginning at the jawbone, trim the throat closely, slightly tapering the hair until it is about $1\frac{1}{2}$ inches long as it approaches the breastbone. Hair below the body at the lower part of the brisket (where the front legs join the body) should be about 2–$2\frac{1}{2}$ inches long. On the sides of the neck the hair should be blended to a roundness and left about two inches long.

6. Blend hair from the occiput into the neck with a trimming knife. Trim the neck evenly down into the back.

7. Trim the back evenly leaving the coat about 2–$2\frac{1}{2}$ inches long. Level the topline right back to the tail.

8. Trim hair on the shoulders evenly down to the front legs.

9. Hair on the front legs should be carefully combed out. Trimming

(preferably with a duplex razor-type knife) should be slight to give a straight line effect, especially on the back of the legs. Sometimes the front and sides of the legs must also be trimmed of excess shaggy hairs to give the desired effect. Cut hair from between toes with a *blunt-nosed* scissors. Shape the paws to roundness with a thinning scissors.

10. The tail should be clipped quite close. The coat on either side of the tail and immediately below should be trimmed sufficiently close to give a sharp outline. This can be done with straight and thinning scissors, or with a #10 blade on the tail and a #4 blade on the rump.

11. Trim the stern of shaggy hairs. Round the rear and blend from short hairs under the tail to a heavier growth at the hocks.

12. Trim and blend from the back to the middle of the thigh. Leave the hair longer and heavier as you work down on the legs.

The stripping knife illustrated in use here is made in Belgium. Its blade is adjustable. There are several variations of this instrument on the market. This one is favored because of its handiness in shortening hair on the top of the head and on the ears. Readers who wish to locate the market for this knife may write to Mrs. Mees in care of the publisher.

Thinning shears are used to trim the hair around the paws so as to make them appear neat and compact. A plain scissors can be used if the points are carefully directed downward.

A dog is usually more comfortable lying down. It is both thoughtful and productive to let him rest while doing those parts of his coat which permit a reclining or sitting position. Remember that a dog's judgements about people are largely based upon tactile response. He can decide if he likes you by your touch because it tells him a great deal about you.

Because the ears of cropped Bouviers are open to air circulation they are less subject to infection. But they are more inclined to get dirty than in flap-eared dogs. The outer ear *only* can be cleaned with a blunt-end tweezer, cotton and alcohol.

Here's a side view of a Bouvier's head groomed for a proud walk—or the show ring.

Grooming finished, Bouvier and groomer celebrate with a handshake.

It's a better relationship all around when a child takes a hand in the care of his dog. Even a very young child can use the combing brush for daily or weekly maintenance. Photo by Walter Chandoha.

The whole idea of grooming is to emphasize Bouvier character and to make the dog more comfortable, cleaner and more welcome in the home. This is Mrs. Carrie Adell's Del-Poppy du Clos des Cerberes.

13. With a trimming knife, lightly even out shaggy hairs from the middle of the thigh to the hock.

14. Trim the backline of the hocks evenly with a scissors and round out the hocks. Cut the hair from between toes and round out the paws.

15. Trim the torso, blending from the shorter hair on the back to a fuller coat at the sides.

16. Trim the underline to show a slight tuck-up from the elbows to the loin. Even out the chest hairs to blend.

Stripping. Periodically some stripping is necessary to remove excess undercoat and allow the outercoat to come through. Keep this problem in check. Do it *once a month!*

1. Brush the torso thoroughly with a slicker brush and comb out with a coarse comb.
2. Back-brush with a pin brush and back-comb with a coarse comb.
3. Back-comb again with a fine comb.
4. Re-brush with the slicker, going only with the grain.

The alternative to monthly stripping is an annual takedown with a stripping knife—a very painful and tedious task.

THE BOUVIER IN OBEDIENCE

THOSE of us who live in complete isolation from other people and their property can please ourselves about whether or not we are going to teach our dogs to be good citizens. Bouviers are big enough, brave enough and powerful enough to become threats to people and property unless they are trained and subjected to reasonable discipline. Fortunately, answers to a potentially difficult problem are at hand.

Dog training is available to anyone. If classes are not offered nearby, any of three or four good books will offer expert guidance.

Under the AKC scheme of things for pure-bred dogs there are four levels of obedience training with titles awarded to dogs proving their competence at each level. "Companion Dog" training covers the basics all dogs need to be good canine citizens: coming, sitting, staying, lying down and stopping on command, heeling on and off the leash and staying in a standing position. Once completed, this training makes a dog a safer, more welcome neighbor. It removes owner fears about getting pulled over by a dog with a tow-pony attitude; it keeps dogs from dashing into streets where they can get killed or cause serious accidents by startling drivers. Consider, also, that a reasonably disciplined dog is a happier dog because he doesn't have to make all of his own decisions—he can feel secure in following the instructions of his "pack leader."

For those who find they especially enjoy training and the competition available at most dog shows there are formal competitions for

She was nearly six months old and her ears were in training tapes. She knew she wanted to go out and she knew how to ask. There was no way of knowing she would go on to win three AKC titles and become the beauty on the right. She's Ch. Deewal Beau Paquet CDX, one of the most accomplished of all Bouviers in America. Photo by Joan Ludwig.

Gentleman Jim Gent's Andre became the second Bouvier in AKC history, and the first male, to earn a Utility Dog title. He is owned by W. Novis Smith of Exton, Pa.

the titles of "Companion Dog Excellent," "Utility Dog" and "Tracking Dog." Almost any Bouvier has the potentiality of achieving all of these titles with the proper training and sufficient opportunities to prove himself in obedience trials.

Obedience competition is quite different from that found in nearby conformation rings. The obedience *handler* is participating to a much greater degree. When things are going right there is thrilling teamwork between handler and dog. Also, dog and handler have three immediate objectives, the most important of which is attainable even if they defeat no other dogs.

First there is the qualifying score to be made. Done three times (only once in tracking) it brings the appropriate obedience degree to the dog. (For members of the American Bouvier des Flandres Club there is a club medal for each obedience title won, just as there is for a conformation champion.)

The next objective of obedience competitors is a high score. Even if it does not bring them a prize it is exciting to see how close to a perfect score of 200 a handler and his dog can get. The third objective is the possibility of getting into the ribbons and prizes.

Many obedience people feel show enthusiasts who haven't tried obedience competition don't know how much more enjoyment they could find in dog shows.

Bouviers are now beginning to achieve their potential in obedience competition. With 1973 records complete at publication time 61 Bouviers had recorded 71 obedience titles. Three of those dogs had three AKC obedience titles each. Four others had two titles each. The first 34 titles took 16 years. The next 37 just four years.

Companion Dog degrees have been recorded by the AKC for 61 Bouviers. Seven of these (four in the last three years) have gone on to earn CDX titles. Only two have progressed on to Utility Dog degrees.[1] Including their achievements in Canadian shows seven of these dogs have won 24 obedience titles. Aldo has seven of these and at publication his owner-trainer-handler, Robert C. Moore of Leamington, Ontario felt the dog was ready to go after the only two left in the U.S. and Canada—the AKC's UD and CKC's OT.

Aldo is the first and only Bouvier to earn the AKC's Tracking Dog title. He holds two Canadian tracking titles, Tracking Dog and Track-

---

1. All, through 1973, are listed in the Appendix.

Her titles, correctly stated are: OT Deewal Merveille UD. She was the AKC's first Bouvier Utility Dog and the second in the records of the Canadian Kennel Club to win the OT degree, roughly the equivalent of a UD. She has won a total of six titles in the U.S. and Canada. She is owned by Mr. and Mrs. F. A. Holmes. Below she does the broad jump.

Ch. Hanover's Chienne D'ore, CD was sired by Urex, below. Both are show and obedience winners.

Ruffkell's Beau Ombre CDX is one of six Bouviers that have won that AKC title. He's owned by Tim and Loryce Heisel of Nanuet, N.Y.

Like Chienne D'ore, above, Ch. Urex Bras de Fer CD belongs to Dr. Clifford and Joyce Bodarky who both enjoy shows and obedience trials.

ing Dog Excellent. With all of his titles it is fortunate he has a short name. Since he is a Canadian dog his Canadian titles are listed first: Aldo, CDX, TDX, U.S. CDX and TD.

Moore states he has trained other breeds including German Shepherds and Doberman Pinschers and that he prefers to work with Bouviers "because once they learn it is not necessary to constantly rehearse them. I just run them through once before we go into the ring and they've got it. I was able to train Aldo for the tracking in five weeks. I started because I was being told Bouviers couldn't take the training and I wanted to prove something. Aldo was only two when he completed his titles. I put another Bouvier, Euro's Heidi, through a Canadian CD but a buyer came along and took her. I've replaced her with a puppy out of Aldo's dam. I've trained some other breeds for other people but I prefer the Bouviers. And, they're so darned good with the kids!"

Aldo was bred by a neighbor of Moore's, Henry van de Bovekamp of Ruthven, Ontario from Troll van de Woolderwei, a Dutch-bred dog out of Villandria's Argena, that made her AKC CD in 1970.

Deewal Merveille UD and OT (Hardy l'Ideal de Charleroi—Deewal Katona) also won six titles for and with her owners, Mr. and Mrs. Frank Holmes of Livonia, Mich. She was the first American UD Bouvier, the second Bouvier to win the equivalent in a Canadian title (the OT), and prerequisite AKC and CKC obedience degrees. She was, of course, also the first AKC Bouvier to win a UD and the first to win both the Canadian and U.S. titles. The Holmeses also trained and handled Deewal Fredrica to American and Canadian CDs.

Gentleman Jim Gent's Andre was the second American UD Bouvier. He qualified in 1970 for W. Novis Smith of Exton, Pa. Merveille had won her AKC UD at Akron, Ohio in 1967, her OT at Oakville, Ontario in 1965 when she was only three.

The others that have progressed to a CDX title are Holda (1956), D'Artagnan le Duc de Maiden in 1966, Ch. Deewal Beau Paquet and Jim and Loryce Heisel's Ruffkell's Beau Ombre in 1971.

Bouviers have achieved so much as police, military and guide dogs and as protector dogs in the United States that their proponents seem not to be fully exploiting their potentialities in obedience competition. In Europe Bouviers have been used in a great variety of services. They are a favorite of the obedience enthusiasts there—and they are here with those who have trained them.

THE BOUVIER IN ART
BY MURRAY HOROWITZ, M.D.

THE Bouvier des Flandres as he presently appears in generally predictable form is so recent a development that exact representations of him can be encountered only in rather recent art expressions. However his identifiable ancestors are sometimes found in a variety of media. Of course the danger here is that the wish to see Bouvier characteristics depicted on the canvas of an old master can foster false belief.

An example might be the fine etching of two dogs by Jan Fyt, 1642. The heads are not unlike the Bouvier's, blocky and rather short muzzled. The bodies are also blocky and strongly built. There are resemblances. But, as a bit of Bouvier history this cannot be called anything more than a "could be." It is better to appreciate such a work for its merit and not try to read significance into it.

There are Bouvier types and transitional ancestors of the breed readily recognizable in occasional artistic expressions of the latter half of the nineteenth century. The etching by Leon Hermann which is reproduced in an earlier chapter is one example. Bronzes by "the Animaliers" with their explicit detail place no strain upon the imagination of those who are looking for undeniable Bouvier characteristics. One of these is illustrated on the next page.

Of course there is always a remote possibility that a definite Bouvier type will be discovered in a very early piece. Certainly even the minor finds each offer some new understanding of the evolution of the Flanders work dogs into our modern Bouvier.

One of the greatest of "The Animaliers," Pierre Jules Mêne (1810-1877), titled his grouping (opposite top) "Dogs Burrowing." The dog in the center has unmistakable Bouvier characteristics. At bottom opposite is a close-up from a different angle of Mêne's signed bronze sculpture. Above are two bronze Bouvier types. They once decorated an 18th-century clock—which accounts for the fact the dog on the right was sculpted with only a part of its right rear leg. There is no documentation on the silver plated plaque below. Again the dogs are undeniable Bouvier types. All are from the collection of Murray and Shirley Horowitz.

The three ceramic Bouviers above were executed by Shirley Horowitz. The plaque of two Bouviers, carved by Ray Marshall, is also in the collection of Murray and Shirley Horowitz.

The etching of two presumably Flemish dogs is by Jan Fyt, 1642. There are some head and body characteristics seen in the modern Bouvier but there is a danger of reading too much into early artistic representations. The carved dog at left is just two inches high and of European origin. The ceramic Bouviers, below, are without documentation. Above pieces from the editor's collection, those below from the Horowitz collection.

The sterling tie clasp and pin (top and bottom) were designed by Carrie Adell, Bouvier breeder and exhibitor. The silver medallion, below was designed by Miss Edmee Bowles who used Ch. Chef de Truffe as her model. It carries the official

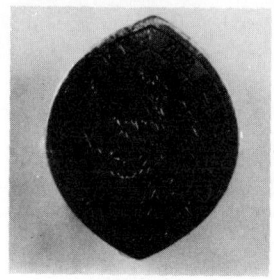

emblem of the American Bouvier des Flandres Club and is presented to owners when their dogs attain championship status or obedience titles. The pin above was once available from the ABFC but the supply has been exhausted. From the Horowitz collection.

CAMPAIGNING THE BOUVIER
BY CHET COLLIER

THOSE of us who believe the Bouvier is the world's finest kind of dog like to see it winning over the other breeds. While it is useful to us to compete within our breed we need the respect of those who do not yet fully appreciate Bouviers. The surest routes to this respect are wins in the group rings—and in the best in show rings.

    The interbreed wins only rarely come to dogs that are shown intermittently. Candidates for group wins should be shown week after week on the better circuits so they can both build and maintain momentum. This means competing in 80 to 125 shows a year.

    There are some matters which must be considered before undertaking such a campaign. You must first of all have a good dog. This may appear to be stating the obvious but there are people who believe a handler can win with a mediocre dog if carefully campaigned. A handler can add only so much. At the top of the competition every other dog has a good handler and any advantage which might accrue to one over the others is negligible. The person who sets his mind to campaigning a dog will find the cost of the best available animal to be his smallest single expense item.

    Take your time. If necessary wait for the right dog. Be businesslike and analytical. Emotional evaluations will almost certainly result in defeat and disappointment.

Next to consider is the choice of a handler. A few owners have developed the skill to compete with the best professionals. Not all of us have the talent or the time to develop it. Nor do many of us have the time for, or the stomach for, constant travel. A few owners enjoy following the show circuits and that is fine for them. They know the best professional handlers could do the job at least equally well and at a fraction of the cost. The professional can carry 12 to 20 dogs as compared to one or two for the circuit-riding amateur.

Like most owners who are out after the group wins or better, I have no choice. My business commitments require that I either utilize a handler or give up the idea of campaigning.

Handling is a very tough and exacting profession. It goes far beyond what is seen in the ring. Not only must the good handler be adept at presenting a dog to judges, he must also have the know-how to keep the dog in top condition (weight, coat, general health, etc.) and, importantly, keep the dog happy and enjoying the showing.

The good handler likes what he does. It is more than just a job. True, he earns his living showing dogs but the good handler thrives on the competition in the show rings. Every time he puts a lead on a dog and parades it for a judge it is with enthusiasm.

It is a plus if a handler has had previous success with your breed. He should at minimum be well experienced with the more nearly similar breeds. He should have the requisite facilities and enjoy the respect of fellow handlers, exhibitors and judges. I prefer a handler who shows sufficiently in my area that I can watch my dog in competition regularly.

The exhibitor who campaigns a dog must have infinite patience. You can't win every time or when you want to. Just as baseball players and golfers have their good and bad streaks, so do dogs. There will be times when you think you will never again win but suddenly everything comes together and it seems your dog can't lose. The exhibitor must learn to live with the highs and lows and take them in stride.

Some people feel that if you are going to campaign a dog it helps to advertise him in the various dog magazines. At one time I thought it was necessary to do this but experience has indicated such advertising is primarily an ego exercise. It does not help winning to the extent that some imagine. The best advertising comes free. If you have

Ch. Raoul des Preux Vuilbaards, owned by Mr. and Mrs. Edward R. Chernoff of New York City, has made some spectacular wins against stiff competition. No one at a show would ever suspect that he is fully attack-trained. Photo by Gilbert

Ch. Raby du Posty Arlequin, owned by W. and B. Dvornik, has been a campaigner consistently placing in working group competition. He is a son of Ch. Quiar de la Thudinie, and a grandson of the illustrious Ch. Naris du Posty Arlequin.

The author showing her Ch. Deewal Benjamen when he was 18 months old. Later, Benjamen proved himself good enough to place in working groups. Photo by Ludwig a good dog presented in good condition members of the dog game will talk about him. You'll find word of mouth is the best advertising possible. Put the money that would go into "see my wonderful dog" advertising into the breeding or purchasing of a good dog. In the long run you will be happier.

ON THE CHARACTER OF THE BOUVIER DES FLANDRES
BY JUSTIN CHASTEL, DE LA THUDINIE KENNELS, THUIN, BELGIUM

THE true nature of the Bouvier des Flandres combined with the selfless utilitarian goals of his breeders has given him a very high and balanced character.

These past years we have confirmed with satisfaction that breeders were ready to give to the Bouvier des Flandres a vigor and a certain perseverance, an individuality which was lacking in the past.

All trainers know it is more agreeable and more feasible to achieve with an alert dog than it is with a lazy dog.

We can then consider the character of the Bouvier is satisfying and that there is nothing to envy in any other breed. We can develop examples and proofs endlessly. After the war of 1914-1918 when amateurs began to become seriously interested in the Bouvier there was in this breed a certain percentage of really ferocious and unmanageable dogs. In my country in most farming areas Bouviers were then kept on chains. At this time the breed held a ferocious reputation.

Since then judicious breeding has eliminated dangerous characteristics. At present the calm and stability of the Bouvier always enchants those who have enough luck to own one of these dogs.

This said, we must carefully guard against losing this heritage and not let it be compromised by insufficiently instructed breeders. In breeding dogs characteristics are quickly set. In only a few generations one can see not only the positive qualities appearing but also the faults. It is, good then, to be forewarned on each matter of character before mistakes are made.

Those in clubs should insist on useful work as a test of Bouvier character.

The Bouvier is nothing of a dandy. Its charm resides in great part in its character. Witness the almost human look through shaggy eyebrows! If it lost this quality what would it have left?

For breeders of Bouviers success will never be complete. There will always be, here and there, individuals of less than true Bouvier character. Regardless of how beautiful or otherwise attractive, such individuals should not be bred from.

All ought to perceive the correct character of the Bouvier des Flandres and look on it as a heritage on which we have no right to infringe, a trust which is ours to enjoy and to pass on unaltered.

Breeders and judges must never forget this obligation.

BOUVIERS IN THE SERVICE OF MAN

THE Bouvier's name is in part a misnomer. The frugal farmers of Flanders evolved him as a utility dog with a specialty. Herding cattle may have been the primary function of the Bouvier and his predecessors but, like farm dogs everywhere, they were expected to contribute by the performance of a wide variety of rural chores.

We have already seen how in their native Flanders Bouviers served as watch and guard dogs, as family companions, as herders of sheep and other livestock in addition to cattle, as destroyers of vermin and even as sometime partners in hunting small game. As cart dogs they have hauled people and produce, dairy and baked goods, traveling tinkers and mobile butcher shops—in fact anything that could be put on wheels and drawn by up to four-dog teams. And it went beyond that. They were even used to power grist mills and to tow canal boats.

In war Bouviers and Bouvier types have served the Belgian military as sentry and Red Cross dogs and even as haulers of machine guns and the wounded. They have been used by Belgian police as patrol and attack dogs. And it will be remembered that the first Bouvier exhibition was restricted to dogs in the service of customs officers—and that their specialty in this service was the capture of smuggler dogs, many of *them* Bouviers, carrying contraband over the border.

The Bouvier's sense of responsibility and property, his concentration and his anxiety to please, his intelligence, his courage and his strength have fitted him well for a great variety of services beyond his nominal role as a herder of cattle.

We have Miss Edmee Bowles' account of how her Bouviers scented out a cache of fifth column ammunition and of how they would give an alert at the approach of German planes before the military warning system knew of the danger. She told of the several times Belco saved her mother and herself during the near-anarchistic stampede of refugees before the advancing Nazis, of how a World War I veteran credited a Bouvier for refusing to leave him for dead on a battlefield. And she told of how Belco, using split second judgement, used himself as a living anchor to save her from a fall down a mountainside.

Louis and Virginia de Rochemont told how their first Bouvier bitch arrived understanding only French but quickly and effectively learned she was being depended upon to warn immediately at the first indication their small son was starting into insulin shock. On a lighter note they also recalled that a Bouvier had played a role in the movie, Outward Bound.

Another Bouvier on the American scene early drew a cart advertising a dog food.

During World War II Bouviers had a greater percentage, by far, of their number serving in the U.S. military than any other breed. Their employment as sentry dogs was chiefly in the Coast Guard's coastal patrol.

The deeper one researches into Bouvier history the more one comes to believe that the tasks the Bouvier hasn't yet accomplished are the ones he hasn't yet been asked to attempt.

Here are some observations on the Bouvier repeatedly encountered in Bouvier research:

1. Under training there seems to be a delay between instruction and response. It is almost as if the Bouvier feels it is necessary to contemplate the advisability of the task assigned him before deciding to accept and execute. Using an idiom of the day, he "gets himself together" before he starts.

2. Once a Bouvier accepts a task as a proper thing for him to do he never challenges it again; he complies quickly and he does not forget.

3. Bouviers are inclined to stick close to home and what they recognize as their responsibilities.

4. The older dogs instruct the young in Bouvier duties.

Bouviers acting as "guiding eyes." All show their tremendous alertness.

5. Because of a strong paternal drive, or whatever, Bouviers tolerate what they seem to recognize as unknowing abuse from children.

6. Like self-appointed foster parents Bouviers will guard and protect their small human charges from anything they deem to be a threat.

7. Most Bouviers exhibit a delicate judgement in responding to threats. If the intimidation of their presence will suffice most will go no further. Louis de Rochemont says his son never lost a playground fight. His Bouvier would gently and firmly grasp any opponent by the seat of his pants and haul the lad out of the fray. A fireman in uniform who approached the de Rochemont home to sell tickets was knocked down and pinned to the ground — but not hurt. Still we know Bouviers can be trained to launch crunching attacks upon command.

The few Bouviers that have had full opportunities to gain the ultimate obedience titles have done very well. The Canadian Bouvier, Aldo, was trained to gain the highest of all tracking titles in just five weeks — and tracking is the specialty of scent hounds, not Bouviers.

In the United States Bouviers serve humans in a variety of roles and we might well examine some of them closely.

The Bouvier as a Guard Dog

In most parts of America crimes of violence have increased sharply in recent years and the dog buying public is more and more focusing on "protection dogs." In fact, many people who would not be otherwise interested in dog ownership have been buying dogs of the larger, more rugged breeds. These do not make good Bouvier owners because people who don't value a dog's companionship beyond what the dog can do for them seldom make successful owners or trainers. A few such "investors" discover the joys of a dog's devotion after the fact but most are incapable of relating to a dog on a mutually happy basis.

There was a controversial article in *Sports Illustrated* magazine based upon an interview with one American breeder. It portrayed the Bouvier as very nearly the ultimate in a guard dog. A pre-existing polarization between Bouvier breeders in North America was exposed by the article's publication. The majority, including most who are interested in conformation competition, felt a gentle-natured breed had been maligned. The minority at the other end felt dog shows would sissify a rugged dog with strong character and great utilitarian

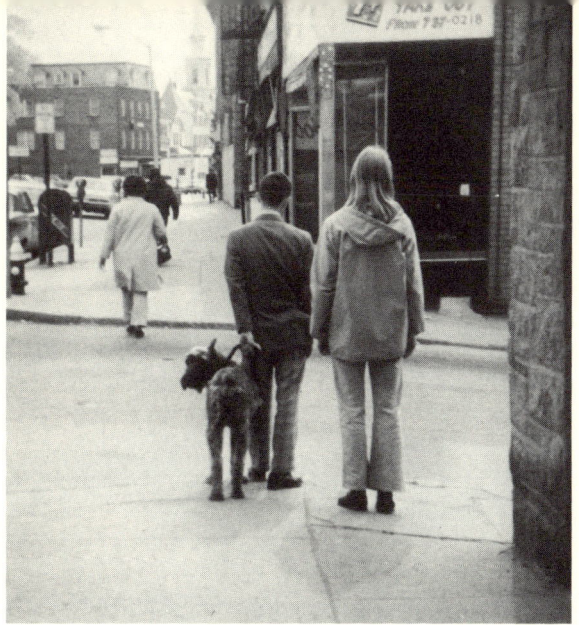

A Guiding Eyes Bouvier and its sightless master grow accustomed to each other on city streets, while a school trainer follows close behind.

potentialities. Under competitive conditions in both the United States and Canada each of the extremes is free to pursue its own direction. Under the Federation Cynologique Internationale guard and attack training is a prerequisite to Bouvier success in the show ring. FCI competitions have conclusively demonstrated the Bouvier can be simultaneously outstanding as a show dog and as an utilitarian dog.

It has also been demonstrated in the United States (where competitions are not interlocked) that continuous breeding in divergent directions over several decades can produce two breeds with a single name and a common ancestry. It has been so with bench and field English Setters and with bench and field Pointers, and with bench and field Beagles, etc. It might be well, therefore, if all Bouvier parties were to reread, and carefully, the counsel of M. Justin Chastel in the chapter immediately preceeding.

In the United States Bouviers have served, and are serving, in police K-9 Corps and with a number of private security agencies. Because service organizations usually fall well short of being high bidders they haven't been acquiring many Bouviers during the period of the breed's ascending popularity. Therefore most Bouviers doing guard duty on this continent are home-protecting family dogs without specialized training.

The Bouvier as a Cattle Dog

The Bouvier arrived in North America a little late to find employment as a drover's dog. A number of excellent breeds had seniority, there was hot new competition arriving from Australia, small farms were disappearing and even the cowboy was finding himself displaced, in part, by helicopters. It is well that the Bouvier has his own charms and other aptitudes.

The Bouvier's classic technique is to move at a fast trot in a semicircle behind his master while focusing on the herd. He is constantly ready to run at any straying beast. He isn't a heeler nipping at his charges. (Heelers get kicked in the head a lot and usually have short careers.) The Bouvier throws body blocks at the fore-end of a cow when necessary—and it is only necessary until that cow has learned to quickly respond to his directions. His method is more akin to that of a springing lion than to a hamstringing wolf.

One Bouvier fancier, Mrs. Christy Comer of Ventura, Calif. utilizes

Above, a Bouvier leaps through a flaming barrier for a Canadian Police officer. Below, a Bouvier serves with a sergeant in the Delray Beach, Fla. Police. (Photo by Stan Sheets)

Above, Bouviers serve as guard dogs in Detroit. The plaque below needs no further testimonial to the ability of Bouviers to serve mankind.

the herding talents of her Bouviers. Her Madrone Ledge Blaise was just a pup when she helped "push" two drop calves and their nurse cows in for milking. Blaise, essentially self-taught, became quite proficient in handling dairy cattle. Mrs. Comer's Deewal Brutus, a big fellow, was able to drive a large bull into its paddock.

Herding training is an on-the-job proposition and the best instructor is usually a skilled older dog. It is hardly the sort of thing any dog can be expected to pick up during a Sunday afternoon on Uncle Frank's farm. That could present some dangers to dog, cattle and property.

Perhaps, someday there will be field trials for herding dogs just as there are for sheepdogs. They would give Bouvier owners incentive to train their dogs and develop ancient talents. There is great joy in watching a dog discover and respond to the instincts of his ancestors. For the dog it is exaltation and adrenalin time. For both handler and dog there is a camaraderie far beyond anything either might experience in any other mutual activity.

The Bouvier and the Blind

Most people have a need to be needed and appreciated. *Some* dogs have those same needs. *Most* Bouviers do. And that is the one biggest reason for their outstanding record as successes in guiding the blind.

It is necessary that a guide dog fully understand the importance of, and respond with dedication to, his duties. Needed is a solid, rather stolid, canine citizen with a strong sense of responsibility and the intelligence to make sound independent judgements.

A further listing of the attributes requisite in a guide dog almost accumulate into a description of a Bouvier. He must be patient, unflappable, brave, capable of adjusting easily to a variety of situations and have the capacity to concentrate upon an assigned task for extended periods of time—then become nearly invisible until called upon again.

Guide dogs must be of a robust, hardy breed, 20 to 26 inches at the shoulder when fully grown. Their coats must be easy to keep clean and to otherwise maintain. The individual dog must be healthy, free of hip dysplasia and without any serious breed blemishes or faults. The guide dog can be neither timid nor aggressive. A pedigree is not necessary and the preferred sex is female.

Most of the dogs in this service have either been bred by the school or donated by their breeders. If donated they cannot be more than two years old and they must have been well socialized to people. Both donated and school-raised puppies are placed with 4-H youngsters for careful care and socialization until they are about ten months old and ready to begin their training programs.

Although there have been outstanding guide dogs of many breeds, those breeds generally preferred, in alphabetical order, are: Alaskan Malamutes, Bouvier des Flandres, Doberman Pinschers, German Shepherds, Golden Retrievers, Labrador Retrievers and mongrels.

All of the eight guide schools are non-profit organizations operating on gifts from the public. They are:

CALIFORNIA

Guide Dogs for the Blind, Inc.
P.O. Box 1200
San Rafael, Calif. 94902

International Guiding Eyes, Inc.
543 Denny Avenue
Hollywood, Calif. 91603

MICHIGAN

Leader Dogs for the Blind
1039 Rochester Road
Rochester, Mich. 48063

MINNESOTA

Master Eyes Foundation of America
509 Produce Bank Bldg.
Minneapolis, Minn. 55403

NEW JERSEY

The Seeing Eye, Inc.
P.O. Box 375
Morristown, N.J. 07960

NEW YORK

Guide Dog Foundation
for the Blind, Inc.
109-19 Seventy-Second Street
Forest Hills, N.Y. 11375

Guiding Eyes for the Blind, Inc.
Granite Springs Road
Yorktown Heights, N.Y. 10598

OHIO

Pilot Dogs, Inc.
625 West Town Street
Columbus, Ohio 43215

One of these, Guiding Eyes for the Blind in Yorktown Heights, N.Y., has had extensive experience with Bouviers. That is because Mgs. Dorothy Walsh, over a period of years, took great satisfaction in donating Bouviers for the Guiding Eyes' program. Today Guiding Eyes breeds most of the dogs it uses. The training is expensive and

Duc, top Belgian attack dog, demonstrates his prowess at a training session.

The Camden, N.J. Police Department has made excellent use of the Bouvier, both in the K-9 Division and for promotion of an anti-jaywalking campaign.

a puppy is ten months old before its training can begin. Therefore each dog rejected after its training begins represents a loss in both time and money. By developing its own strains of Labradors and Golden Retrievers the school hopes to constantly reduce the incidence of rejections and simultaneously intensify those genetic characteristics it finds most desirable. The breeding program is producing both consistency and high acceptability. Nevertheless, Bouviers are especially welcome at Guiding Eyes because they have been star pupils and extremely effective after their graduation. Only one of the first 39 had to be rejected (for hip dysplasia).

Bouviers have one important advantage over Labs, Boxers and Goldens. It is deterrent quality. Unfortunately, there are some who prefer to steal from the blind. A blind person traveling about a city needs a guide dog that *looks* like a capable protector and that can, if necessary, *be* an effective protector.

At the invitation of Geoffrey Lock, director of Guiding Eyes, the author spent a day there. It was an impressive and rewarding experience.

A Bouvier, Deewal Charm, just one year old, had been assigned to her new master a week earlier and I had an opportunity to watch them learning to work and live together.

Our entourage set out to test the streets of the city of Peekskill, N.Y. Charm's master was in his early thirties, an upright, quick stepping chap with obvious confidence in Charm and in himself. Their instructor, a young lady, followed a couple of paces to the rear. Fifty or more feet further back Mr. Lock, a photographer and I followed. Our first responsibility was not to interfere.

Each time the team approached a dangerous obstacle I was tempted to voice a warning—but there was no need. The first was an open cellar door in the middle of the sidewalk. Charm picked a path between the hazzard and the curb. Next came three exuberant and noisy small boys racing down the sidewalk on their bikes. Charm paused and stood her ground until they passed. On command she resumed. Next there was a street to cross. They stopped at the curb. The man stepped forward until he could feel the curb with his feet. Expertly judging the traffic flow by sound, he commanded "forward" and they crossed safely. At another intersection Charm refused the "forward." There was a right-turning car. When the street was safe she proceeded.

Next they encountered a man using an electric saw. Lumber and sawhorses were arranged like a labyrinth. The carpenter looked up, saw the blind man and Charm approach—and went right on with his work. I thought he was crass and unfeeling. Mr. Lock must have read my thoughts. He explained that the people of Peekskill were used to such situations and encouraged by the school to just go on with their business.

Charm and the young man next proceeded up a hill. The sidewalk was composed of uneven blocks, presumably to make it negotiable in slippery weather. Soon their progress was slowed by two elderly ladies inching their way up. To pass them Charm would either have to take to the street or cross a lawn. She evaluated the situation neatly and took the lawn route—with some delicate timing.

The temptations of the next hazzard can only be fully appreciated by dog-wise people. A hound noticed their approach and trotted out to the sidewalk. As the blind man and Charm approached he stiffened and bristled. Charm ignored him completely, striding right past him. There was one more busy intersection to negotiate. Then we all returned to the school.

Charm's new master had to describe his almost-solo to the other students gathered. Each bragged on his or her dog and I am sure each had reason to do so.

Mr. Lock told me his is the only school which undertakes to help the blind who have a second major handicap. He told of a deaf girl who has written back: "Rego hears for me now." A young man with cerebral palsy discovered his Guiding Eye dog not only guided his footsteps but steadied them. And, doesn't that suggest a new area of service by dogs such as Bouviers to people who have difficulty moving or maintaining their balance?

No Guiding Eye Bouvier has ever failed on the job. None has ever had to come back for a refresher course or any other reason—except one.

Arga, a spayed bitch was teamed with an American Indian youth. Together they went to a South Dakota reservation to live. Peter Iron Mountain and the big daughter of Ch. Argus de la Thudinie had been first in their graduation class at Guiding Eye. On the reservation they lived happily for several years. Peter Iron Mountain, no longer helpless, enjoyed a new respect in his community. Pranksters who had teased him before learned to respect Arga.

Peter Iron Mountain's mother wrote the school explaining why she was returning Arga. Peter had gone joy riding in a fast car with other youths. He was killed in a crash. At first Agra waited by the door for his return. She refused food. Later, as was her custom, she lay by his bed with her head across his old shoes. At night she began lifting her head to the skies and howling—almost wolflike. Still she wouldn't eat. Fearing Arga might die too, the grieving mother shipped her back to Guiding Eyes. Arga was thin, weakened and still mourning when she arrived in Yorktown.

By then Arga was too old to be assigned to a new student. Lock refused to entertain thoughts of putting her to sleep. He called Mrs. Walsh and asked if she could help. Fourtunately the mistress of Deewal knew just the right home for Arga. A friend, the artist and illustrator, Kurt Wiese, had a great love for dogs—and room for another at his rural studio-home in Frenchtown New Jersey. Perhaps it was the complete change of environment, or the tender, loving care. More likely it was both, but Arga today lives happily. She stays close to Wiese though—just in case he has need of a guiding eye.

BOUVIER RECORDS AND STATISTICS, COMPILED BY CARL B. MAY, JR.

Ours is a young enthusiasm. It is only a little more than forty years since the first Bouvier was registered with the American Kennel Club and since the first was exhibited at an American show. It has been less than twenty years since Bouviers became known to more than a handful of breed boosters in North America.

While we continue to be dependent upon importations for the improvement of our strains it is encouraging to note that American-bred Bouviers are more and more winning their share of the shows and trials. Now, while our history is more ahead of us than behind us, it is well to record here the achievements of Bouvier pioneers of today and earlier, to commit to print the achievements of importers, breeders, exhibitors, trainers—and their Bouviers. These records will provide us with a measuring stick of our progress. The common goal of American Bouvier des Flandres Club members is the constant improvement of our dogs. Each *new* record will be an indicator that we are progressing, that we are producing better and better Bouviers.

American Bouvier Des Flandres Club
Specialty Winners

1965: Kennel Club of Philadelphia
    BOB Ch. Konard du Rotiane
    BOS Ch. Giaconda du Clos des Cerberes
1966: Kennel Club of Philadelphia
    BOB Ch. Job de la Thudinie
    BOS Ch. Deewal la Belle de Belgique
1967: Kennel Club of Philadelphia
    BOB Ch. Deewal Lorenzo
    BOS Ch. Aurega du Clos des Cerberes
1968: Kennel Club of Philadelphia
    BOB Ch. Naris du Posty Arlequin
    BOS Ch. Odelette du Posty Arlequin
1969: Kennel Club of Philadelphia
    BOB Ch. Odelette du Posty Arlequin
    BOS Ch. Blandford's Raoel
1970: Sand and Sea Kennel Club, New Jersey
    BOB Ch. Prudhon des Preux Vuilbaard
    BOS Ch. Deewal Altesse
1970: Kennel Club of Philadelphia
    BOB Ch. Picolette du Posty Arlequin
    BOS Ch. Naris du Posty Arlequin
1971: Westchester Kennel Club
    BOB Ch. Jasper du Clos des Cerberes
    BOS Ch. Sia du Posty Arlequin
1971: Kennel Club of Philadelphia
    BOB Ch. Madrone Ledge Socrates
    BOS Ch. Tamara Bras de Fer
1972: Somerset Hills Kennel Club
    BOB Ch. Tamara Bras de Fer
    BOS Ch. Quiar de la Thudinie
1973: Harrisburg Kennel Club
    BOB Ch. Tamara Bras de Fer
    BOS Ch. Sir Jumbo du Clos des Cerberes
1974: Detroit Kennel Club
    BOB Ch. Deewal Victor
    BOS Ch. Dominique du Clos des Cerberes

BOUVIER FIRSTS AND RECORDS TO BE BROKEN

First Bouvier registered with the AKC:	Hardix, 1931
First Bouvier exhibited in the U.S.A.:	Laddie, owned by P. O'Brien of Old Westbury, N.Y. Bred by G. McCullough (Hardix-Diane de Montreuil) at Westminster KC, N.Y.C., 1931.
First to win a group placement:	Ch. Marius du Clos des Cerberes, AKC A-744749
First bitch to win a group placement:	Si Jolie du Clos des Cerberes
First to attain an AKC championship:	Ch. Bojar van Westergoo, June 10, 1939
First bitch to attain an AKC championship:	Ch. Lisa AKC A224994, 1943
First to win a working group first placement:	Ch. Coquin de la Thudinie
First to win best in show:	Ch. Argus de la Thudinie
First bitch to win best in show:	Ch. Picolette du Posty Arlequin
First to win more than one best in show:	Ch. Naris du Posty Arlequin
First American-bred AKC champion:	Ch. Marius du Clos Cerberes
First best of breed at an American Bouvier des Flandres Club specialty:	Ch. Konrad du Rotiane
First American-bred to win best in show:	Ch. Madrone Ledge Socrate
First American-bred to win a working group first placement:	Ch. Deewal Lorenzo

First American-bred bitch to win a working group first:	Ch. Tamara Bras de Fer
First littermates to win AKC championships:	Ch. Ciskoldo, Ch. Riasta and Ch. Ellydria
First breeder of record:	Julius Bliss
First to qualify for an AKC obedience degree:	Astra-Yerta W98090, 1954
First to qualify for the obedience degree, "companion dog excellent:"	Deewal Merveille UD, Can. OT
First to qualify for the obedience degree, "utility dog:"	Deewal Merveille UD, Can. OT
First to qualify for the obedience degree, "tracking dog:"	Aldo CDX, TD, Can. CDX and TDX
First to attain an AKC championship on the west coast:	Ch. Ciskoldo
First bitch to attain an AKC championship on the west coast:	Ch. Riasta
First champion to qualify for an obedience degree:	Ch. LaBette de la Cucarde CD
First west coast champion to qualify for an obedience degree:	Ch. Deewal Beau Paquet CDX
First AKC champion to qualify for the obedience degree, "companion dog excellent:"	Ch. D'Artagnan le Duc de Maidan CDX
First to place in the working group on the west coast:	Ch. Deewal Benjamen
First American-bred to win best in show in Canada:	Ch. Blandford's Basko
First handler-breeder-judge:	Mrs. Patricia Marcmann
First male, second to earn AKC obedience title, "utility dog:"	Gentleman Jim Gent's Andre UD

First to win both AKC and Mexican titles:	Ch. and Mex. Ch. Zorina du Clos des Cerberes
First to win AKC, Candian and Mexican championships:	Ch., Can. and Mex. Ch. Redfox Liberty Bell
First Bermudian, Mexican and AKC champion:	Ch., Ber. and Mex. Ch. Konard du Rotiane
First to qualify for the obedience degree "companion dog" in the U.S., Canada and Bermuda:	Ch. Redfox Smokie, CD, Can. and Ber. CD
First to win championships in both the U.S. and Canada:	Ch. and Can. Ch. Deewal Argusue CD
Largest litter whelped and reported—18 puppies, three still-born, Aug., 1962:	Ch. Kaline du Posty Arlequin (to Ch. Erlo de la Thudinie)
Youngest to win an AKC championship—4 majors, 19 points at 8 months, 11 days:	Ch. Vlaanderen I'm Kelli Too
Oldest to win an AKC championship—9 years, 5 months, 15 days:	Ch. Argus de la Thudinie
Most outstanding record in AKC shows:	Ch. Naris du Posty Arlequin
Most outstanding record in AKC shows for an American-bred:	Ch. Bibarcy's Soldat de Plomb
Most outstanding record in AKC shows for a bitch:	Ch. Picolette du Posty Arlequin
Most outstanding record in AKC shows for an American-bred bitch:	Ch. Tamara Bras de Fer

Top Twenty Bouviers des Flandres, AKC Competitions, 1932 through 1972. Rating by the number of Bouviers defeated

Name	Best of Breeds	Bouviers defeated	Av. Bouv. def. per BB	Rank by def. per BB
1. Naris du Posty Arlequin	179	312	1.74	19
2. Prudhon des Preux Vuilbaards	93	281	3.02	13
3. Konard du Rotiane	65	273	4.2	5
4. Deewal Lorenzo	77	258	3.35	10
5. Hion de la Thudinie	75	241	3.21	11
6. Deewal Benjamen	104	223	2.14	17
7. Argus de la Thudinie	64	200	3.12	12
8. Picolette du Posty Arlequin	84	198	2.35	15
9. Tamara Bras de Fer	40	168	4.2	5
10. Raby du Posty Arlequin	82	163	2.0	18
11. Job de la Thudinie	44	156	3.54	8
12. Boris v d Ouden Dijk CD	41	141	3.44	9
13. Bibarcy Soldat de Plombe	104	134	1.29	20
14. Odelette du Posty Arlequin	17	117	6.88	1
15. Tristan du Clos des Cerberes	26	116	4.46	4
16. Marc de la Thudinie	29	107	3.7	7
17. Madrone Ledge Socrate	45	106	2.35	15
18. Quiar de la Thudinie	16	84	5.25	2
19. Coquin de la Thudinie	92	72	0.76	21
20. Hanover's Alon	13	64	4.92	3
20. Banquo du Clos des Cerberes	22	64	2.91	14

Rating systems are helpful but a single factor system, or double at left, can be misleading. Multiple factor systems introduce the problem of properly weighting the factors. The chart's rankings on the left, for example, are drastically altered (see column on the right) when the function of the two rated factors is computed. Undoubtedly other winners would have to be included if all Bouviers were to be rated as in the right hand column. There are unseen factors. Ch. Coquin de la Thudinie, for example, was being shown, mostly in the midwest at a time when he was often the first Bouvier ever exhibited in the area. Owner Joan Butts was promoting the breed by displaying a good Bouvier without thought of establishing records.

For a variety of reasons some good dogs get more opportunities to win than do others. Bitches, particularly if matrons, average significantly fewer show opportunities. A more enthusiastic or more prosperous owner can make a difference. A dog can suffer an injury early in its show career, or a persistent skin problem can hold it back. owners living near population centers can more easily get to shows.

Top AKC Show Winning Bouviers By Year

Name	Breeder	Owner	Bouv Def.	BOB	Group Placements I	II	III	IV	BIS
		1965							
1. Ch. Konard du Potiene	Adams	Neylon	129	27	1	3	2	4	1
2. Ch. Deewal Lorenzo	Deewal	Currie	95	31	1	1	1	3	
3. Ch. Job de la Thudinie	Neylon	Thiele	19	4				1	
4. Ch. De Ney's Grosse Knabe	Chastel	Deewal	35	9		1		1	
		1966							
Ch. Konard du Rotiane	R. Adams	Neylon	92	25	1	3	3	4	
Ch. Deewal Lorenzo	Deewal	Currie	49	19	1	1	2	2	
Ch. Job de la Thudinie	Chastel	Deewal	41	4					
Ch. Redfox Lariat CD	Markham	Markham	26	12					
Ch. Deewal Beauregard	Deewal	Marcus	19	4					
Ch. Boris v.d. Ouden Dijk	Van Vorst	Miller	12	8					
Ch. Schandor du Clos des Cerberes	Bowles	Bowles	10	1					
Frisia's Tawney Miss	Prinsen	Morin	7	2					
Ch. Redfox Clonmel	Markham	Markham	7	3					
Ch. Deewal Desiree	Deewal	Hallerman	7	2					
Madrone Ledge Masker	Hubbard	Hubbard	6	3					
Ch. Deewal Yvette	Deewal	Deewal	5	1					
Ch. Marc de la Thudinie	Chastel	Abady	5	2					
		1967							
Ch. Deewal Lorenzo	Deewal	Currie	81	13	1	1		2	
Ch. Job de la Thudinie	Chastel	Deewal	49	11			2	1	

Name	Sire	Dam							
Ch. Boris v.d. Ouden Dijk CD	von Vorst	Miller	42	10					2
Ch. Tristan du Clos des Cerberes	Bowles	Cook	40	7					
Ch. Redfox Lariat CD	Markham	Markham	24	13					
Ch. Marc de la Thudinie	Chastel	Abady	19	3					
Ch. Konard du Rotiane	Adams	Neylon	16	2					
Deewal Tristan	Deewal	Deewal	14	4					
Deewal Daniel	Deewal		13	2					
Ch. Nic de Ney	Neylon		12	2					
Ch. Schandor du Clos des Cerberes	Bowles	Bowles	11	2					
Ch. Deewal Beauregard	Deewal	Marcus	11	2					
Ch. Picard des Preux Vuilbaards	Abady	Menken	8	3					
Ch. Deewal Grand Prix	Horowitz	Horowitz	8	3					

1968

Name	Sire	Dam							
Ch. Naris du Posty Arlequin	Grulois	Collier	91	33	7	4	4		
Ch. Boris v.d. Ouden Dijk CD	Von Vorst	Miller	87	23	1	1	1	4	1
Ch. Marc de la Thudinie	Chastel	Abady	72	22	4	4	1	3	1
Ch. Odelette du Posty Arlequin	Grulois	Hubbard	41	12			1	3	
Ch. Prudhon des Preux Vuilbaard	Abady	Mees	41	12	1			2	
Ch. Zorina du Clos des Cerberes	Bowles	Rutherford	29	16					
Ch. Job de la Thudinie	Chastel	Deewal	21	15		1	1	3	
Ch. Bibarcy's Job's Daughter	Deewal	Pedersen	27	5					
Ch. Bibarcy's Gendarme	Pedersen	Pedersen	27	4					
Ch. Genius Teddy Boo Bear	Beckwith	Parker	16	4					

Name	Breeder	Owner	Bouv Def.	BOB	Group Placements				BIS
					I	II	III	IV	
		1969							
Ch. Naris du Posty Arlequin	Grulois	Collier	148	78	11	21	12	4	2
Ch. Prudhon des Preux Vuilbaard	Abady	Mees	74	33	4	3	2	4	
Ch. Raoul des Preux Vuilbaard	Abady	Chernoff	15	6			1	1	
Ch. Odelette du Posty Arlequin	Grulois	Hubbard	62	3					
Ch. Qarlo Segundo De Ney	Neylon	Neylon	14	2		1		1	
Ch. Picolette du Posty Arlequin	Grulois	Hubbard					1		
Ch. Quiar de la Thudinie	Chestel	Deewal	14	5				3	
Ch. Tgauchsin Machque	Deewal	Lepic					1		
		1970							
Ch. Prudhon des Preux Vuilbaards	Abady	Mees	24	94	3	4	4	1	
Ch. Picolette du Posty Arlequin	Grulois	Hubbard	38	88	3	5	4	1	
Ch. Naris du Posty Arlequin	Grulois	Collier	68	87	18	8	9	10	7
Ch. Deewal Benjamen	Deewal	Deewal	46	76			1	4	
Ch. Bibarcy's Soldat de Plomb	Pedersen	Pedersen	11	46					
Ch. Banquo du Clos des Cerberes	Bowles	Rutherford	16	16					
Ch. Tgauchsin Machque	Deewal	Lepic	20	28					
Ch. Quiar de la Thudinie	Chastel	Deewal	6	27					
Ch. Redfox Smokie CD	Markham	Markham	9	24					
Ch. Blandford's Basko	Miller	Miller	3	18					
Ch. Blandford's Nicholas	Miller	Herec	6	18					
		1971							
Ch. Picolette du Posty Arlequin	Grulois	Hubbard	43	107	2	3	5	6	1
Ch. Deewal Benjamen	Deewal	Deewal	36	98		3	1	1	
Ch. Raby du Posty Arlequin	Grulois	Collier	51	82	6	3	10	6	1

Name								
Ch. Prudhon des Preux Vuilbaards	Abady	Mees	24	59		2	2	3
Ch. Madrone Ledge Socrate	Hubbard	Hubbard	19	57	2			2	1
Ch. Tamara Bras de Fer	Mees	Mees	15	41	1			
Ch. Quiar de la Thudinie	Chastel	Deewal	3	31			1	
Ch. Madrone Ledge Tamboryn	Hubbard	Weaver	10	30				
Ch. Bougie de Fau Allure	Rosenberg	Herec	6	28				1
Ch. Bibarcy's Soldat de Plomb	Pedersen	Pedersen	20	21				1
Ch. Sasa des Preux Vuilbaards	Abady	Pedersen	11	28				

1972

Name								
Ch. Tamara Bras de Fer	Mees	Mees	122	24		3		
Ch. Raby du Posty Arlequin	Grulois	Collier	92	39	6	6	4	5	2
Ch. Bibarcy's Soldat de Plomb	Pedersen	Pedersen	64	62	20	14	11	5	6
Ch. Madrone Ledge Socrate	Hubbard	Hubbard	54	29		3	1	3
Ch. Hanover's Alon	Bodarky	Bodarky	47	11				
Ch. Jasper du Clos des Cerberes	Bowles	Bowles	42	4				
Ch. Trajan des Preux Vuilbaards	Abady	Medefessor	42	11				
Ch. Deewal Benjamen	Deewal	Deewal	32	13		1		
Ch. Terry du Posty Arlequin	Grulois	DeLanda	20	3				
Ch. Prudhon des Preux Vuilbaards	Abady	Mees	19	2			1	1
Ch. Ruffkell's Delight	Goldman	Levy					1	1
Ch. Taquin du Posty Arlequin	Grulois	Collier				3	1	1
Ch. Quiar de la Thudinie	Chastel	Deewal	1			1		

AKC Obedience Degree Holders

AKC UTILITY DOG DEGREES
Deewal Merveille, can. OT	1967
Gentleman Jim Gent's Andre	1972

AKC TRACKING DOG DEGREE
Aldo CDX, TD, Can. CDX and TDX	1971

ADDITIONAL AKC COMPANION DOG EXCELLENT DEGREES
Ch. D'Artagnan le Duc de Maidan	1966
Ch. Deewal Beau Paquet	1971
Holda	1956
Ruffkell's Beau Ombre	1972

ADDITIONAL AKC COMPANION DOG DEGREES
Astra-Yerta	1954
Athena de Lagonisi	1971
Beau Andre de Green Henge	1971
Beau Garth Asgard	1970
Beau's Gentle Ben	1970
Bibarcy's Spook	1973
Bras de Fer Undine	1973
Ch. Boris v d Ouden Dijk	1966
Ch. De Ney's Argus Marteau D'or	1965
Ch. Deewal Argusue	1964
Ch. Deewal Beulah II	1966
Deewal Blitzen	1973
Ch. Deewal Calant de Charlaire	1969
Deewal Entre Nous	1965
Deewal Fredrica	1971
Deewal Gabriel d'Artois	1966
Deewal Jobey Junior	1970
Deewal Luc Triomphe de Carole	1971
Deewal Manifique	1967
Deewal Maurice du Plateau	1968
Deewal Owyhee Brogan	1969
Deewal Shane Du	1968

Ch. Electra du Clos des Cerberes	1970
Fantome du Clos des Cerberes	1973
Flanette d'Pranhky	1966
Grenadier Alida O'River Oakes	
Greycliff's Kimo	1973
Guerrire Obscurite des Ghent	1969
Hanover's Alon	1972
Hanover's Chienne D'or	1973
Je T'Adore	1971
Ch. Jez Zaa Bell	1970
Joey the Rascal of Haal	1969
Ch. La Bete de la Cucarde	1958
L'Etoille Quoridienne Bennett	1969
Ch. Lisa	
Liska du Clos des Cerberes	1972
Maidan's Cavalier Tigre	1967
Maidan's Truffelyn	1967
Pandora des York	1967
Quantasoi Vuilbaard de Ney	1968
Ch. Redfox Lariat	1970
Ch. Redfox Smokie	1967
Ch. Redfox Velvet Lassie	1967
Roxanne's Beau	1967
Roxanne's Carlo Rex A'dele	1968
Sia du Posty Arlequin (B)	1971
Silta II	1958
Tasha Bras de Fer	1972
Tasja of Argena	1972
Titus du Pti Blond	1972
Ch. Urex Bras de Fer	1973
Usbe des Preux Vuilbaards	1972
Villandria's Argena	1970
Zabeth	1973

COMPLETE LISTING OF THE 204 BOUVIERS DES FLANDRES COMPLETING AKC CHAMPIONSHIPS, 1931-1973

AKC CHAMPION	DATE	SIRE	DAM
Altair du Clos des Cerberes (11-70)	1970	Ch. Schandor du Clos des Cerberes	Ch. Aurega du Clos des Cerberes
Andelane's Simone (2-73)	1973	Picolo de la Thudinie (B)	Cambo's Yvette
Argus de la Thudinie (B)	1959	Volpi de la Vallee de Ecaillon (B)	Ucaba de la Thudinie
Asgard Bravado	1971	Ch. Pebbles du Posty Arlequin (B)	Ch. Deewal la Belle de Belgique
Aurega du Clos des Cerberes	1967	Ch. Telstar du Clos des Cerberes	Deewal Marzie Lamb
Babette de Saint Roch	1971	Ch. Redfox Smokie CD	Blandford's Bianca
Babka de Saint Roch (1-72)	1971	Ch. Redfox Smokie CD	Blandford's Bianca
Banquo du Clos des Cerberes (3-70)	1971	Ch. Schandor du Clos des Cerberes	Gaea du Clos des Cerberes
Bel Echo du Clos des Cerberes	1957	Ch. Marius du Clos des Cerberes	Ch. Ellydria
Bianca du Clos des Cerberes	1973	Ch. Jaspar du Clos des Cerberes	Ch. Pallas du Clos des Cerberes
Bibarcy's Casandra (8-70)	1969	Deewal Demon Ripp	Ch. Bibarcy's Job's Daughter
Bibarcy's Casanova	1968	Deewal Demon Ripp	Ch. Bibarcy's Job's Daughter
Bibarcy's Fashionette	1971	Deewal Demon Ripp	Ch. Bibarcy's Job's Daughter
Bibarcy's Gendarme	1968	Deewal Demon Ripp	Ch. Bibarcy's Job's Daughter
Bibarcy's Job's Daughter (2-68)	1968	Ch. Job de la Thudinie (B)	Ch. Deewal Argusette
Bibarcy's Petite Patrice	1968	Deewal Demon Ripp	Ch. Bibarcy's Job's Daughter
Bibarcy's Solitaire	1971	Ch. Deewal Ringo	Bibarcy's Guinevere
Bibarcy's Soldat de Plomb	1970	Ch. Deewal Homer	Ch. Bibarcy's Job's Daughter
Bibarcy's Songuese	1971	Ch. Deewal Homer	Ch. Bibarcy's Job's Daughter
Bibarcy's Symphonie (6-72)	1973	Ch. Deewal Ringo	Bibarcy's Angelique
Bibarcy's Tambour de Ville	1971	Ch. Pebbles du Posty Arlequin (B)	Ch. Deewal la Belle de Belgique
Bibarcy's Tourterelle (9-68)	1971	Ch. Pebbles du Posty Arlequin (B)	Ch. Bibarcy's Casandra
Blandford's Audrie	1973	Ch. Boris v d Ouden Dijk CD (N)	Leida Herta v d Ouden Dijk (N)
Blandford's Bolto	1971	Ch. Boris v d Ouden Dijk CD (N)	Penny the Pooh
Blandford's Basko	1970	Ch. Boris v d Ouden Dijk CD (N)	Penny the Pooh
Blandford's Julia Van	1973	Ch. Blandford's Raoel	Andrea de Uer (5-71)
Blandford's Nicholas	1969	Ch. Boris v d Ouden Dijk CD (N)	Penny the Pooh

236

Blandford's Raoel	1969	Ch. Boris v d Ouden Dijk CD (N)	Penny the Pooh
Blandford's Rudo (8-73)	1972	Ch. Boris v d Ouden Dijk CD (N)	Penny the Pooh
Blandford's Toby	1973	Ch. Blandford's Raoel	Miss Boleyn (3-72)
Bodres Baron of Greycliff	1973	Ch. Blandford's Rudo	Greycliff's Tina
Bojar van Westergoo (N) (Black)	6-10-39	Kamboro (N)	Alexandrina Olga van Marberg (N)
Bonaparte v Darling Astrid (N) (12-52)	1953	Altor (N)	Elisa Alieda v d Zaanhoeve (N)
Boris v d Ouden Dijk CD (N) (7-67)	1967	Amoroh (N)	Herta Carla v d Ouden Dijk (N)
Bougie de Fer Allure	1971	Ch. Prudhon des Preux Vuilbaards	Ranni Bras de Fer
Bras de Fer Ursa	1973	Ch. Prudhon des Preux Vuilbaards	Oriane des Preux Vuilbaards (4-69)
Briska du Clos des Cerberes	1962	Bel Ami du Clos des Cerberes	Yhelot
Cal-Grons Baldur Noup van Dafzicht (N)	1973	Noup de la Thudinie (B)	Yulca van Dafzicht (N)
Caramel Truffe	1960	Ch. Coquin de la Thudinie (B)	Ch. Draga de la Thudinie (B)
Chanterie Redfox Venti	1973	Ch. Prudhon des Preux Vuilbaards	Ch. Ripeau Bras de Fer
Chanterie Vicaire	1973	Ch. Prudhon des Preux Vuilbaards	Ch. Ripeau Bras de Fer
Charlemagne de Harris	1973	Ch. Deewal Thor	Ch. Madrone Ledge Tamboryn
Chef de Truffe	1961	Ch. Coquin de la Thudinie (B)	Ch. Draga de la Thudinie (B)
Ciskoldo (Brindle)	1952	Basko Alieda v d Zaanhoeve (N)	Silta (N)
Coquin de la Thudinie	1956	Ygor des Courdreaux (F)	Zola de la Thudinie (B)
Dante of Grey Mer	1962	Hardy l'Ideal de Charleroi (B)	Asta l'Ideal de Charleroi
D'Artagnan le Duc de Maidan CDX	1966	Ch. Chef de Truffe	Ch. Briska du Clos des Cerberes
Deewal Altesse (2-63)	1968	Ch. Deewal Lorenzo	Ch. Irca de la Thudinie (B)
Deewal Argusette	1960	Ch. Argus de la Thudinie (B)	Ch. Fausette l'Ideal de Charleroi (B)
Deewal Arguson	1962	Ch. Argus de la Thudinie (B)	Ch. Fausette l'Ideal de Charleroi (B)
Deewal Argusue CD (11-62)	1961	Ch. Argus de la Thudinie (B)	Ch. Fausette l'Ideal de Charleroi (B)
Deewal Beau Paquet CDX	1972	Ch. Job de la Thudinie (B)	Ch. Deewal Argusue CD
Deewal Beauregard	1966	Ch. Job de la Thudinie (B)	Compeer Paulette
Deewal Benjamen	1970	Ch. Job de la Thudinie (B)	Ch. Deewal Altesse
Deewal Beulah II CD	1967	Hardy l'Ideal de Charleroi (B)	Ch. Deewal Argusue CD
Deewal Bianca	1959	Bel Ami du Clos des Cerberes	Yhelot

Deewal Bonne Amie	1962	Ch. Argus de la Thudinie (B)	Ch. Deewal Nicole
Deewal Calant d'Charlaire CD (12-73)	1973	Ch. Job de la Thudinie (B)	Ch. Deewal Argusette
Deewal Claudette	1965	Hardy l'Ideal de Charleroi (B)	Ch. Deewal Argusue CD
Deewal Desiree	1967	Ch. Hion de la Thudinie (B)	Ch. Deewal Georgiana
Deewal Estioc Mon Ami Pierrot	1961	Ch. Argus de la Thudinie (B)	Ch. Deewal Nicole
Deewal Georgiana	1964	Hardy l'Ideal de Charleroi (B)	Ch. Deewal Argusette
Deewal Grand Prix	1965	Hardy l'Ideal de Charleroi (B)	Ch. Deewal Argusue CD
Deewal Hardisse (8-65)	1964	Ch. Deewal Arguson	Compeer Paulette
Deewal Hion	1966	Ch. Hion de la Thudinie (B)	Ch. Deewal Georgiana
Deewal Homer (B, imp. in utero)	1971	Kous de la Thudinie (B)	Perette de la Thudinie (B)
Deewal la Belle de Belgique	1965	Ch. Deewal Arguson	Ch. Deewal Nicole
Deewal Lady Argus	1965	Hardy l'Ideal de Charleroi (B)	Ch. Deewal Argusette
Deewal Lorenzo	1964	Hardy l'Ideal de Charleroi (B)	Ch. Deewal Argusette
Deewal Lucette	1970	Deewal Demon Ripp	Ch. Deewal Yvette
Deewal Nicole	1960	Etoile des Courdreaux (F)	Trixie
Deewal Nomura	1967	Ch. Hion de la Thudinie (B)	Ch. Deewal Georgiana
Deewal Ringo (5-70)	1971	Ch. Job de la Thudinie (B)	Ch. Deewal Altesse
Deewal Samantha	1967	Ch. Deewal Grand Prix	Ch. Deewal Hardisse
Deewal Taikoun	1962	Ch. Caramel Truffe	Deewal Argus Lass
Deewal Thor (2-73)	1972	Ch. Quiar de la Thudinie (B)	Deewal Johanna
Deewal Thunderbluff	1973	Ch. Quiar de la Thudinie (B)	Flanette Jemina (5-72)
Deewal Toronto	1958	Ch. Bonaparte v Darling Astrid	Ch. Deewal Zita
Deewal Victor (B, imp. in utero)	1973	Tapin de la Thudinie (B)	Ch. Silette de la Thudinie (B)
Deewal Yvette	1966	Ch. Job de la Thudinie (B)	Compeer Paulette
Deewal Zita	1959	Bel Ami du Clos des Cerberes	Yhelot
Del Poppy du Clos des Cerberes	1965	Ch. Chef de Truffe	Ch. Remado's Katleen (B)
De Landa's Nemo (2-70)	1971	Frisia's Bob	Nanay du Clos des Cerberes
De Ney's Argus Marteau D'or CD	1967	Ch. Hion de la Thudinie (B)	Ch. Remado's Jasmine (B)
De Ney's Grosser Knabe	1965	Ch. Hion de la Thudinie (B)	Ch. Remado's Jasmine (B)

Dom'nique du Clos des Cerberes	1973	Ch. Roland du Clos des Cerberes
Draga de la Thudinie (B)	1959	Ch. Argus de la Thudinie (B)
Duxbury House's Ulrich	1972	Ch. Prudhon des Preux Vuilbaards
Electra du Clos des Cerberes CD	1963	Ch. Rostan du Clos des Cerberes
Eliane du Clos des Cerberes (4-67)	1965	Ch. Chef de Truffe
Ellydria	1953	Basko Alieda v d Zaanhoeve (N)
Erlo de la Thudinie (B)	1959	Ch. Argus de la Thudinie (B)
Fausette l'Ideal de Charleroi (B)	1960	Bonzo l'Ideal de Charleroi (B)
Genius Teddy Boo Bear	1968	Ch. Job de la Thudinie (B)
Gentleman Jim Gent (8-62)	1963	Ch. Caramel Truffe
Giaconda du Clos des Cerberes	1964	Ch. Chef de Truffe
Glad-Stan's Barabbas	1971	Ch. Banquo du Clos des Cerberes
Glad-Stan's Maria	1971	Ch. Banquo du Clos des Cerberes
Grenadier Coquette of Walden	1969	Grenadier Alfrego de la Vons
Gretel of Frisia	1967	Deewal Arguson
Hanover's Alon	1972	Ch. Prudhon des Preux Vuilbaards
Hanover's Ardanne	1972	Ch. Prudhon des Preux Vuilbaards
Hanover's Beatrix	1973	Ch. Jaspar du Clos des Cerberes
Hanover's Belle Amie	1973	Ch. Jaspar du Clos des Cerberes
Hilgrand Georgette	1974	Ch. Quiar de la Thudinie (B)
Hilprize Kelli Sandra (10-70)	1971	Ch. Job de la Thudinie (B)
Hion de la Thudinie (B)	1962	Cendrillo de L'ile Monsin (B)
Irca de la Thudinie (B)	1963	Hardy l'Ideal de Charleroi (B)
Iseult du Clos des Cerberes	1968	Ch. Chef de Truffe
Jaspar du Clos des Cerberes (8-72)	1971	Brabo du Clos des Cerberes
Jez Zaa Bell CD (6-72)	1972	Deewal Brutus
Jo Mo Kenyatta (2-74)	1973	Gabriel de la Terres
Job de la Thudinie (B) (2-64)	1964	Ch. Hion de la Thudinie
Kaline du Posty Arlequin (B)	1963	Ch. Hion de la Thudinie (B)

		Ch. Altair du Clos des Cerberes
		Canaille de la Thudinie (B)
		Ch. Ronni des Preux Vuilbaards
		Grenadier Alida O'River Oakes CD
		Ch. Remado's Katleen (B)
		Silta (N)
		Zolla de la Thudinie (B)
		Asta l'Ideal de Charleroi (B)
		Ch. Deewal Beulah II CD
		Deewal Doone
		Sapho du Clos des Cerberes
		Ch. Zorina du Clos des Cerberes
		Ch. Zorina du Clos des Cerberes
		Coquette de la Thudinie (B)
		Frisia's Hertha II
		Ch. Sarita du Clos des Cerberes
		Ch. Sarita du Clos des Cerberes
		Ch. Hanover's Ardanne
		Ch. Hanover's Ardanne
		Deewal Nimiety of Bromorc
		Ch. Deewal Hardisse
		Demoiselle de la Thudinie (B)
		Demoiselle de la Thudinie (B)
		Ch. Remado's Katleen (B)
		Ch. Altair du Clos des Cerberes
		Madrone Ledge Blaise
		Ax la Chapelle
		Hulotte de la Thudinie (B)
		Iota du Posty Arlequin (B)

Katrien du Clos des Cerberes	Ch. Marius du Clos des Cerberes	1956
Konard du Rotiane (B)	Bonzo l'Ideal de Charleroi (B)	1964
Krespie de la Thudinie (B)	Ch. Job de la Thudinie (B)	1965
La Bete de la Cucarde CD	Ch. Coquin de la Thudinie (B)	1959
Laska's April Mist	Ch. Madrone Ledge Terpodian	1973
Le Boof de Chardonnay	Anaris du Pontier (11-71)	1973
Lillie's Veettee	Rhombus des Preux Vuilbaards	1973
Lisa (Black, whelped 9-30-37)	Ch. Bojar van Westergoo (N)	1943
Madrone Ledge Renni	Ch. Naris du Posty Arlequin (B)	1970
Madrone Ledge Socrate (11-72)	Ch. Naris du Posty Arlequin (B)	1971
Madrone Ledge Tamboryn (2-73)	Ch. Quiar de la Thudinie (B)	1971
Madrone Ledge Taussant	Ch. Quiar de la Thudinie (B)	1973
Madrone Ledge Terpodian	Ch. Quiar de la Thudinie (B)	1972
Madrone Ledge Tosca (12-72)	Ch. Quiar de la Thudinie (B)	1972
Madrone Ledge Troll	Ch. Quiar de la Thudinie (B)	1971
Madrone Ledge Valmur	Ch. Madrone Ledge Socrate	1973
Madrone Ledge Venus	Ch. Madrone Ledge Socrate	1973
Madrone Ledge Viking	Ch. Prudhon des Preux Vuilbaards	1973
Maidan's Alvin	Ch. Konard du Rotiane (B)	1969
Marc de la Thudinie (B)	Ch. Job de la Thudinie (B)	1968
Marius du Clos des Cerberes (Black)	Belco	1949
Naris du Posty Arlequin (B)	Ch. Marc de la Thudinie (B)	1968
Nic de Ney	Ch. Konard du Rotiane (B)	1967
Nikos Kazantzakis (9-72)	Ch. Deewal Homer (B)	1972
Ninette de la Thudinie (B)	Lais du Posty Arlequin (B)	1969
Noceur de la Thudinie (B) (7-68)	Lais du Posty Arlequin (B)	1969
Nota du Posty Arlequin (B)	Lais du Posty Arlequin (B)	1967
Odelette du Posty Arlequin (B) (3-68)	Moka de la Thudinie (B)	1968
Ola du Clos des Cerberes (4-72)	Ch. Marc de la Thudinie (B)	1971

	Ch. Ellydria
	Hosca l'Ideal de Charleroi (B)
	Iatte de la Thudinie (B)
	Ch. Katrien du Clos des Cerberes
	Jacqueline K (8-72)
	Grenadier Lady Annissa (11-71)
	Ricca des Preux Vuilbaards
	Coba uit het Zuiderlicht (N)
	Madrone Ledge Masker
	Pepita du Posty Arlequin (B)
	Ch. Odelette du Posty Arlequin (B)
	Ch. Odelette du Posty Arlequin (B)
	Ch. Odelette du Posty Arlequin (B)
	Ch. Odelette du Posty Arlequin (B)
	Ch. Odelette du Posty Arlequin (B)
	Ch. Madrone Ledge Renni
	Madrone Ledge Tigrette (9-72)
	Ch. Odelette du Posty Arlequin (B)
	Ch. Giaconda du Clos des Cerberes
	Remado's Kitty (B)
	Ch. Lisa
	Johane du Posty Arlequin (B)
	Ch. Remado's Jasmine (B)
	Ch. Bibarcy's Job's Daughter
	Hermine de la Thudinie (B)
	Hermine de la Thudinie (B)
	Lolo du Posty Arlequin (B)
	Liska du Posty Arlequin (B)
	Ch. Eliane du Clos des Cerberes

Name	Sire	Year	Dam
Pallas du Clos des Cerberes (12-70)	Ch. Schandor du Clos des Cerberes	1969	Ch. Eliane du Clos des Cerberes
Pebbles du Posty Arlequin (B) (9-68)	Olaf de la Thudinie (B)	1968	Linouche du Posty Arlequin (B)
Pepita du Posty Arlequin (B) (1-69)	Olaf de la Thudinie (B)	1968	Linouche du Posty Arlequin (B)
Perrette du Maidan de Ney	Ch. Konrad du Rotiane (B)	1967	Ch. Giaconda du Clos des Cerberes
Pica des Preux Vuilbaards	Ch. Marc de la Thudinie (B)	1969	Ch. Nota du Posty Arlequin (B)
Picard des Preux Vuilbaards (3-68)	Ch. Marc de la Thudinie (B)	1967	Ch. Nota du Posty Arlequin (B)
Picolette du Posty Arlequin (B)	Ch. Naris du Posty Arlequin (B)	1970	Ch. Odelette du Posty Arlequin (B)
Pouky de L'ile Monsin (B)	Omsky de L'ile Monsin (B)	1971	Kata de L'ile Monsin (B)
Prince v Young	Duke von Young	1965	Arendine
Prudhon des Preux Vuilbaards (4-69)	Ch. Marc de la Thudinie (B)	1968	Ch. Nota du Posty Arlequin (B)
Qarlo Segundo de Ney	Ch. Konard du Rotiane (B)	1969	Ch. Remado's Jasmine (B)
Quiar de la Thudinie (B) (5-70)	Ch. Naris du Posty Arlequin (B)	1969	Nia de la Thudinie (B)
Quina de la Thudinie (B)	Ch. Naris du Posty Arlequin (B)	1969	Nia de la Thudinie (B)
Raby du Posty Arlequin (B)	Ch. Quiar de la Thudinie (B)	1971	Lolo du Posty Arlequin (B)
Raoul des Preux Vuilbaards	Ch. Noceur de la Thudinie (B)	1969	Mouche du Posty Arlequin (B)
Redfox Clonmel	Ch. Rostan du Clos des Cerberes	1965	Ch. Deewal Bonne Amie
Redfox Lariat CD	Ch. Rostan du Clos des Cerberes	1965	Ch. Deewal Bonne Amie
Redfox Liberty Bell	Ch. Picard des Preux Vuilbaards	1971	Ch. Redfox Velvet Lassie CD
Redfox Smokie CD (12-71)	Ch. Redfox Clonmel	1969	Jingles of Blueberry Bank
Redfox Velvet Lassie CD	Ch. Rostan du Clos des Cerberes	1967	Ch. Deewal Bonne Amie
Redfox Whisp of Smoke	Ch. Redfox Smokie CD	1973	Sia du Posty Arlequin (B)
Remado's Jasmine (B)	Ike de Belgique (B)	1964	Irisa de L'ile Monsin (B)
Remado's Katleen (B)	Ike de Belgique (B)	1965	Irisa de L'ile Monsin (B)
Riasta (Black) (Whelped 9-27-47)	Basko Alieda v d Zaanderhoeve (N)	1952	Silta (N)
Ripeau Bras de Fer (7-72)	Ch. Prudhon des Preux Vuilbaards	1971	Oriane des Preux Vuilbaards
Roland du Clos des Cerberes (5-72)	Ch. Telstar du Clos des Cerberes	1973	Ch. Pallas du Clos des Cerberes
Ronni des Preux Vuilbaards	Ch. Marc de la Thudinie (B)	1970	Onega des Preux Vuilbaards
Rostan du Clos des Cerberes	Bel Ami du Clos des Cerberes	1960	Si Jolle du Clos des Cerberes
Rostansa du Clos des Cerberes	Ch. Schandor du Clos des Cerberes	1970	Ch. Aurega du Clos des Cerberes

Rouette des Preux Vuilbaards		1970	Ch. Marc de la Thudinie (B)	Onega des Preux Vuilbaards
Ruffkell Delight		1972	Flanette Ruff	Ch. Hilprize Kelli Sandra
Sadine du Posty Arlequin (B)		1971	Rasquin de la Thudinie (B)	Rumba du Posty Arlequin (B)
Sasa des Preux Vuilbaards		1971	Ch. Noceur de la Thudinie (B)	Racha des Preux Vuilbaards
Sarita du Clos des Cerberes (2-71)		1969	Ch. Picard des Preux Vuilbaard	Ch. Eliane du Clos des Cerberes
Schandor du Clos des Cerberes		1966	Ch. Chef de Truffe	Ch. Remando's Katleen (B)
Scherif des Preux Vuilbaards (8-71)		1971	Ch. Noceur de la Thudinie (B)	Racha des Preux Vuilbaards
Sibon des Preux Vuilbaards		1971	Ch. Noceur de la Thudinie (B)	Onega des Preux Vuilbaards
Silette de la Thudinie		1973	Rico de la Thudinie (B)	Quelly de la Thudinie (B)
Sir Jumbo du Clos des Cerberes		1972	Brabo du Clos des Cerberes (B)	Ch. Eliane du Clos des Cerberes
Tamara Bras de Fer		1970	Ch. Prudhon des Preux Vuilbaards	Oriane des Preux Vuilbaards
Taquin du Posty Arlequin (B)		1972	Rico de la Thudinie	Praline du Posty Arlequin
Taurus du Clos des Cerberes (6-70)		1973	Brabo du Clos des Cerberes	Ch. Ola du Clos des Cerberes
Tgauchsin Machque		1971	Ch. Job de la Thudinie (B)	Ch. Deewal Altesse
Telstar du Clos des Cerberes		1966	Ch. Rostan du Clos des Cerberes	Ch. Remado's Katleen (B)
Terri Bras de Fer (12-71)		1972	Ch. Prudhon des Preux Vuilbaards	Oriane des Preux Vuilbaards
Terry du Posty Arlequin (B)		1971	Rico de la Thudinie (B)	Praline du Posty Arlequin (B)
Thias des Preux Vuilbaards (8-71)		1972	Rhombus des Preux Vuilbaards	Regine de la Thudinie (B)
Timlor Vitalite		1973	Ch. Quiar de la Thudinie (B)	Ch. Hilprize Kelli Sandra
Toro van Dafzicht (N)		1973	Bica v d Rozenheerd (N)	Astra Noup v Dafzicht (N)
Trajan des Preux Vuilbaards		1972	Rhombus des Preux Vuilbaards	Regine de la Thudinie (B)
Tristan du Clos des Cerberes		1963	Ch. Chef de Truffe	Sapho du Clos des Cerberes
U Oliver des Preux Vuilbaards		1973	Ch. Noceur de la Thudinie (B)	Taquine des Preux Vuilbaards
Ullya des Preux Vuilbaards		1973	Ch. Noceur de la Thudinie (B)	Regine des Preux Vuilbaards
Ur des Preux Vuilbaards		1973	Rhombus des Preux Vuilbaards	Taquine des Preux Vuilbaards
Uraine des Preux Vuilbaards		1973	Rhombus des Preux Vuilbaards	Rachea des Preux Vuilbaards
Urex Bras de Fer CD		1972	Ch. Prudhon des Preux Vuilbaards	Ranni Bras de Fer
Uriah Bras de Fer		1973	Ch. Prudhon des Preux Vuilbaards	Ranni Bras de Fer
Uris Bras de Fer		1972	Ch. Prudhon des Preux Vuilbaards	Ranni Bras de Fer
Valois des Preux Vuilbaards		1973	Ch. Noceur de la Thudinie (B)	Taquin des Preux Vuilbaards

Walden's Etranger		1965	Grenadier Alfrego de la Vons	Kara du Posty Arlequin (B)
Zorina du Clos des Cerberes (3-70)		1968	Ch. Chef de Truffe	Ch. Remado's Katleen (B)
Zorra du Clos des Cerberes		1957	Bel Ami du Clos des Cerberes	Elfrida du Clos des Cerberes

(B) Bred in Belgium. (F) Bred in France. (N) Bred in The Netherlands. Figure, as (12-73), in parentheses indicates date of *AKC Stud Book* in which dog's registration is published. (This information not complete here.) Color, where known, is indicated in parentheses for earlier champions. The first twelve AKC champions were: Bojar van Westergoo that completed at the North Westchester show under Lewis S. Worden for owner George W. Young, Jr. in an entry of five Bouviers on June 10, 1939; Ch. Lisa for Dorothy S. Young in 1943; Marius du Clos des Cerberes for Miss Edmee Bowles in 1949; the littermates bred by Evert van de Pol, Ciskoldo and Riasta in 1952 and Ellydria in 1953; Bonaparte v Darling Astrid in 1953; Coquin de la Thudinie and Katrien du Clos des Cerberes in 1956; Bel Echo du Clos des Cerberes and Zorra du Clos des Cerberes in 1957—and Deewal Toronto in 1958. Half of these were owned, at one time or another, by Miss Bowles. During their first 28 years under the AKC Bouviers averaged less than one champion every two years. From 1959 through 1973 they averaged almost 13 a year. In 1973 a total of 39 Bouviers completed AKC championships.

Rankings of Actively Competing Bouviers, by Bouviers defeated, as reported by the AKC covering dates, Oct. 22, 1972 through Dec. 16, 1973

Rank	Name	Best of Breeds	BIS	Bouv. Defeated	Group Placements I	II	III	IV	Av. Bouv. Def. per BB	Rank by Average
1.	Ch. Taquin du Posty Arlequin	56	2	320	11	15	8	6	5.71	5
2.	Ch. Sir Jumbo du Clos des Cerberes	21		106					5.05	8
3.	Ch. Uriah Bras de Fer	28		100	2	5	3	4	3.57	10
4.	Ch. Tamara Bras de Fer	12		80	1	2	2	1	6.66	4
5.	Ch. U Oliver des Preux Vuilbaards	21		80	0	11	4	1	3.81	9
6.	Ch. Bibarcy's Soldat de Plomb	22		44	5	7	3	1	2.00	12
7.	Ch. Glad-Stan's Barabbas	6		42					7.00	3
8.	Ch. Pouky de l'Ile Monsin	3		40					13.33	1
9.	Ch. Bodres Baron of Greycliff	5		26					5.20	7
10.	Ch. Madrone Ledge Socrate	3		22					7.33	2
10.	Ch. Silette de la Thudinie	4		22					5.50	6
10.	Ch. Trajan des Preux Vuilbaards	8		22					2.75	11
†	Ch. Raby du Posty Arlequin					1	1			
†	Ch. Duxbury House's Ulrich							1		

(†) Not in top ten in Bouviers defeated but had group placements.

While these statistics in part overlap those in the "all-time top 20" (covers competition through 1972), they suggest continual revisions in those rankings will have to be made. Rapid changes occur because increasing registrations result in mounting show entries. In 1973 over 16% of all the Bouviers registered by the AKC during the 48 years its books have been open to the breed were entered. That's nearly eight times the annual

APPENDIX

Pedigrees

Pedigrees are most useful to breeders who have seen and studied the dogs and who have knowledge of their genetic qualities. It is hardly possible for one person to gain such intimate knowledge about more than a few dogs. But, even novices can learn much from studies of dog ancestries.

Pedigrees tell much about how the most accomplished breeders did the trick. In Bouviers particularly there has been extensive line breeding, a great deal of it out of necessity—first to establish the breed and then in successive recoveries from wars.

Examination of the French and Belgian ancestral charts reveals consistent line, or family, breeding with judicious crosses to kennels which have chosen similar directions for their breeding programs. Close cooperation between such as Florian Verbanck and Justin Chastel and later between Chastel and Felix Groulois has produced the world's most successful Bouviers. Yet both de la Thudinie and du Posty Arlequin continue to reach out for qualities they admire in other Belgian and French kennels.

One person cannot have an intimate knowledge of all of the dogs in his kennel unless: (1) he confines himself to roughly two dozen or fewer breeding age dogs; (2) he actively seeks comparison under competitive conditions with the best available; (3) he keeps his genetic inventory in an unscrambled, comprehensible form by staying rather close to the lines he knows best.

A serious breeder should have the courage to go outside his kennel to wherever there is stock which might benefit his breeding program. And, he should strive to be on good terms with others in his breed so he *can* cooperate with them.

BELCO, male, whelped Nov. 21, 1935, breeder - H. D. Halm, Kesteren

```
                Brigand des Goujons      Cesar
            Brigand                      Astade la Surete
                Nitouche                 Hiberina's Sancho
        Arie van het Polderleven         Lea
                Dragon Astrid van Maarland   Bel. Ch. Francoeur de Liege
                Belladonna Zea van'y Falkland   Astrid ora van Maarland
                Zea Lotte van Maarland   Pic de la Loutre
                                         Mary Pickford du Pandore
```

BELCO   AKC 96039, NHSB 45565

```
                Cuno                     Zigoto Belga van de Scharrebier
            Baldusar                     Dragette van Arnwald
                Dragette van Arnwald     Milton
        Gardenia                         Rebeke
                Alexio                   Felix van de Haemstede
            Elsionora                    Hibernia's Draga
                Dessa van de Hunzestad   Zambo van Eindhoven
                                         Zea Lotte van Maarland
```

CH. BOJAR VAN WESTERGOO, male, whelped June 23, 1936, Breeder - J. Ferwerda

```
                Felix van de Haemstede   Buston du Vieil Breaut
            Ajax                         Cora de la Jidelidad
                Meda                     Sultan
        Neth. Ch. Kamboro, NHSB 24563    Bianca van de Haemstede
                Zambo van Eindhoven      Samlo
            Dessa van de Hunzestad       Badin van Bindhoven
                Zea Lotte van Maarland   Pic de la Loutre
                                         Mary Pickford du Pandore
```

CH. BOJAR VAN WESTERGOO, AKC A94841

```
                Bello van Eschsicht      Max du Vieil Escaut
            Albert Boa van de Bietebauw  Zampa Ora van Maarland
                Boa Belga van Maarland   Max du Vieil Escaut
        Alexandrina Olga van Marberg, NHSB 30628   Belga de la Gendarmerie
                Hibernia's Pacho         Samlo
            Hibernia's Olga              Liza
                Dainty van Arnwald       Milton
                                         Rebeka
```

CZARDAS VAN HET BUNDERBOSCH, AKC A412320, male, whelped Sept. 30, 1938
    Breeder, M. Widdershoven

```
                Bouboule de Courtrai     Boby du Sellier
            Faro Astrid van Maarland     Arga de la Lys
                Astrid Ora van Maarland  Max du vieil Escaut
        Neth. Ch. Athos Allette de Teugenaar   Ora de la Loutre
                Max du Vieil Escaut      Davros de la Lys
            Allette Belga van Maarland   Riga
                Belga de la Gendarmerie  Dragon de la Lys
                                         Lary
```

CZARDAS VAN HET BUNDERBOSCH, AKC A412320

```
                Zambo van Eindhoven      Samlo
            Zambo Uit het Zuiderlicht    Badin van Eindhoven
                Irmada                   Louis
        Ganesa Uit het Zuiderlicht       Lydia
                Dulo van Arnwald         Ch. Milton
            Norma                        Rebeka
                Florence                 Zado Belga van de Scharrebier
                                         Arizona
```

CH. ROSTAN DU CLOS DES CERBERES, AKC W915224, male, whelped May 22, 1958
    Breeder - Miss Edmee Bowles

```
            Belco                              Arie van het Polderleven
     Ch. Marius du Clos des Cerberes           Gardenia
            Ch. Lisa                           Ch. Bojar van Westergoo
  Bel Ami du Clos des Cerberes                 Coba uit het Zuiderlisht
        Ch. Baska Aleida du Zaanhoeve          Neth. Ch. Athos Allette de Teugenaer
     Ch. Ellyrdia                              Aleida Santa van de Zaanhoeve
            Silta                              Dormento
                                               Arina Ivana van Lexmonde
```

CH. ROSTAN DU CLOS DES CERBERES

```
     Jan du clos des Cerberes                  unknown
            Dombey                             unknown
            Inga                               unknown
  Si Jolie du Clos des Cerberes                unknown
     Samos des Trois Ilses                     Jaf du Chateau de Villiers
            Wandru des Coudreaux               Rita de la Geulardiere
        Bel. Ch. Uada du Gratte Saule          Ravachol
                                               Silane de la Thudinie
```


BONAPARTE VAN DARLING-ASTRID, AKC W321377, male, whelped Apr. 23, 1950
    Breeder - H.L.M. Veugelers

```
         Duvel Bellona van de Zaanhoeve        Neth. Ch. Max Simba van Sappemee
         Carlo van Heems Kerk                  Bellona Aleida van de Zaanhoeve
            Feronia                            Neth. Ch. Basko Aleida van de Zaanhoeve
   Altor                                       Hiandra
            Gerfaut                            Zonnax
         Dorminta                              Fleur
            Krynica                            Aldeharan
                                               Styria
```

BONAPARTE VAN DARLING-ASTRID

```
     Neth. Ch. Athos Allette de Teugehaar      Faro-Astrid van Maarland
         Lagoa uit het Zuiderlicht             Allette Belga van Maarland
     Neth. Ch. Argonda van het Bunderbosch     Gabari du Bungaliow
  Elisa Aleida van de Zaanhoeve                Ganesa uit het Zuiderlicht
     Neth. Ch. Kamboro                         Ajax
         Aleida Santa van de Zaanhoeve         Dessa van de Hunzestad
            Santa                              Neth. Ch. Fred-Bea van Maarland
                                               Uda
```


ARGUS DE LA THUDINIE, male, whelped May 30, 1951, breeder, J. Chastel

```
         Azor de la Boheme, LOF 1 Bouv 119     Erix
     Bel. Ch. Quasimodo, LOF 1 Bouv 115        Yann de Loos
         Meg de la Boheme, LOF 1 Vouv 1056     Isidore de la Boheme
  Volpi de la Vallee de l'Ecaillon, LOF 1 Bouv 3438 Orangine de la Boheme
         Quarl, LOF 1 Bouv 1007                Poker
     Sapho, LOF 1 Bouv 1530                    Mirette de la Chapelle Boby
         Rapsie de la Planque, LOF 1 Bouv 987  Olof de la Sapiniere
                                               Monna
```

CH. ARGUS DE LA THUDINIE, LOSH 159075, AKC WA13921

```
         Joris du Ble d'Or, LOSH 76351         Gollino
     Int. Ch. Soprano de la Thudinie, LOSH 113156  Eprise du Beryl
         Mirette de la Thudinie, LOSH 95153    Lucifer de la Thudinie
  Ucaba, LOSH 128447                           Albionne de Biercee
         Kiou del Roque du Moulin, LOSH 82249  Gascon du Pont Royal
     Rakina de la Thudinie, LOSH 109891        Hermanie del Roque du Moulin
         Mirette de la Thudinie, LOSH 95153    Lucifer de la Thudinie
                                               Albionne de Biercee
```

CH. NARIS DU POSTY ARLEQUIN, male, whelped Aug. 27, 1964, breeder - F. Grulois

        Ch. Hion de la Thudinie   Cendrillo de l'Ile Monsin
    Ch. Job de la Thudinie   Demoiselle de la Thudinie
        Hulotte de la Thudinie   Bonzo l'Ideal de Charleroi
  Ch. Marc de la Thudinie   Flambee de la Thudinie
        Ike de Belgique   Fricko de Belgique
    Remado's Kitty   Erna de Belgique
                  Ch. Ely
        Irissa de l'Ile Monsin   Balta de l'Ile Monsin

CH. NARIS DU POSTY ARLEQUIN

                  Int. Ch. Soprano de la Thudinie
        Ver l'Ideal de Charleroi Reine l'Ideal de Charleroi
    Bonzo l'Ideal de Charleroi   Salvin
        Xanthane   Ugenia
  Johane du Posty Arlequin   Volpi de la Vallee de l'Ecaillon
    Ch. Argus de la Thudinie   Ucaba
    Eliane de la Thudinie   Ygor des Coudreaux
        Canaille de la Thudinie Zolla de la Thudinie

ETOILE DES COUDREAUX, AKC W669477, male, whelped May 17, 1955, breeder - Mme A. Sornin de Leysat

                  Azor de la Boheme
    Bel. Ch. Quasimodo   Meg de la Boheme
  Voulzzi de la Boheme   Quinio du Grand Sauzay
    Uniqueo de la Boheme   Raani
Azor dit Axoum de Pierre Sereine   Sherif des Trois Iles
    T'Joel des Trois Iles   Sonia des Trois Iles
  Vani de Grandin   L'Ami de la Boheme
    Sirene de Grandin   Naja de Mont Glonne

ETOILE DES COUDREAUX

                  Int. Ch. Soprano de la Thudinie
    U'Felon de la Thudinie   Albi
  Whist du Bois des Salues   Kadour de la Romanee
    Rina de Neubourg   Jade de la Romanee
Antinea des Coudreaux   Jaf du Chateau de Villers
    Samos des Trois Iles   Rita de la Gueulardiere
  Wanda des Coudreaux   Ravachol
    Bel. Ch. Uada du Gratte   Silane de la Thudinie
        Saule

ALBIONNE DU DEC, AKC W689369, female, whelped Sept. 11, 1955, breeders - Joan and Robert P. Butts, Jr.

                  Int. Ch. Soprano de la Thudinie
    U'Felon de la Thudinie   Albi
  Ygor des Coudreaux   Samos des Trois Iles
    Ch. Wanda des Coudreaux   Ch. Uada du Gratte Saule
Ch. Coquin de la Thudinie   Joris du Ble d'Or
    Int. Ch. Soprano de la Thudinie Mirette de la Thudinie
  Zolla de la Thudinie   Int. Ch. Soprano de la Thudine
    Ucaba   Rakina de la Thudinie

ALBIONNE DU DEC, AKC W689369

                  Arie van de Polderleven
    Belco   Gardenia
  Ch. Marius du Clos des Cerberes Ch. Bojar van Westergoo
    Ch. Lisa   Coba uit den Zuiderlicht
Katrien du Clos des Cerberes
    Neth. Ch. Basko Aleida van de Zaanhoeve Neth. Ch. Athos Allette de Teugenaar
                  Aleida Santa van de Zaanhoeve
  Ellyrdia   Dormento
    Silta   Arina Ivana van Lexmonda

ERLO DE LA THUDINIE, AKC W983499, male, whelped Oct. 12, 1955, breeder
J. Chastel

```
                                        Azor de la Boheme
            Quasimodo                   Meg de la Boheme
       Volpi de la Vallee de L'Escaillot
            Sapho                       Quarl
    Ch. Argus de la Thudinie            Rapsie de la Planque
       Int. Ch. Soprano de la Thudinie  Joris du Ble d'Or
                                        Mirette de la Thudinie
       Ucaba
          Rakina de la Thudinie         Kiou del Roque du Moulin
                                        Mirette de la Thudinie
```

ERLO DE LA THUDINIE

```
                                        Gollino
         Joris du Ble d'Or              Eprise du Beryl
       Int. Ch. Soprano de la Thudinie  Lucifer de la Thudinie
         Mirette de la Thudinie         Albionne de Biercee
    Zolla de la Thudinie                Joris du Ble d'Or
       Int. Ch. Soprano de la Thudinie  Mirette de la Thudinie
       Ucaba
         Rakina de la Thudinie          Kiou del Roque du Moulin
                                        Mirette de la Thudinie
```

POLAX, AKC W73559, male, whelped Aug 25, 1942, breeder - L. de Rochemont

```
                                            Bouboule de Coutrai
         Faro-Astrid van Maarland            Astrid Ora van Maarland
       Neth.Ch. Athos Allette de Teugenaar
         Ailette Belga van Maarland          Max du Vieil Escaut
    Czardas van het Bunderbosch              Belga de la Gendarmerie
         Zambo uit het Zuiderlicht           Zambo van Eindhoven
       Ganesa uit het Zuiderlicht            Irmada
         Norma                               Dulo van Arnwald
                                             Florence
```

POLAX

```
                                            Ajax
         Neth.Ch. Kamboro                   Dessa van de Hunzestad
       Ch. Bojar van Westergoo
         Alexandrina Olga van Marberg       Albert Boa van de Biete Brauw
    Coba, AKC A501408                       Hibernia's Olga
         Zambo van Eindhoven                Samlo
       Coba uit het Zuiderlicht, AKC A95907 Baden van Eindhoven
         Irmada                             Louis
                                            Lydia
```

CH. HION DE LA THUDINIE AKC WA222599, male, whelped Dec. 2, 1958
breeder J. Chastel

```
                                            Int. Ch. Soprano de la Thudinie
         Tito                               Rakina de la Thudinie
       Urmin du Gratte-Saule
         Silane de la Thudinie              Nick du Ballieux
    Cendrillo de L'Ile Monsin               Mirette de la Thudinie
         Quinto                             Khedive du Gabari
       Tamia de L'Ile Monsin                Kobra de Beaufays
         Reine de Lac-Aux Dames             Jarnac de Beaufays
                                            Ilotanie
```

CH. HION DE LA THUDINIE

```
                                            Bel.Ch. Quasimodo
         Volpi de la Valee deL'Escaillot    Sapho
       Ch. Argus de la Thudinie
         Ucaba                              Int. Ch. Soprano de la Thudinie
    Demoiselle de la Thudinie               Rakina de la Thudinie
         Ygor des Coudreaux                 Felon de la Thudinie
       Canaille de la Thudinie              Fr. Ch. Wanda des Coudreaux
         Zolla de la Thudinie               Int. Ch. Soprano de la Thudinie
                                            Ucaba
```

250

CH. KONARD DU ROTIANE, AKC WA419253, male, whelped May 27, 1961
    breeder - R. Adams

```
                                        Joris du Ble d'Or
            Int. Ch. Soprano de la Thudinie
                                        Mirette de la Thudinie
      Ver L'Ideal de Charleroi          Kari du Beryl
      Reine L'Ideal de Charleroi        Merveille
 Bonzo L'Ideal de Charleroi             Intoly
      Salvin                            Riquette
 Xanthane                               Int. Ch. Soprano de la Thudinie
      Ugenia                            Tosca
```

CH. KONARD DU ROTIANE

```
                                        Volpi de la Vallee de L'Ecaillon
      Ch. Argus de la Thudinie          Ucaba
 Ch. Erlo de la Thudinie                Int. Ch. Soprano de la Thudinie
      Zolla de la Thudinie              Ucaba
 Hosca L'Ideal de Charleroi             Ver L'Ideal de Charleroi
      Bonzo L'Ideal de Charleroi        Xanthane
      Civette L'Ideal de Charleroi      Int. Ch. Soprano de la Thudinie
      Kimenie L'Ideal de Charleroi      Rokine L'Ideal de Charleroi
```

CH. COQUIN DE LA THUDINIE, AKC W605220, male, whelped Oct. 10, 1953
    breeder - J. Chastel

```
                                        Joris du Ble d'Or
            Int. Ch. Soprano de la Thudinie
                                        Mirette de la Thudinie
      U'Felon de la Thudinie            Unknown
      Albione de Biercee                Unknown
 Ygor des Coudreaux                     Jaf du Chateau de Villers
      Samos des Trois Iles              Rita de la Gueulardiere
 Wanda des Coudreaux                    Ravachol
      Bel. Ch. Uada du Gratte-Saule     Silane de la Thudinie
```

CH. COQUIN DE LA THUDINIE

```
                                        Gollino
      Joris du Ble d'Or                 Eprise du Beryl
 Int. Ch. Soprano de la Thudinie        Lucifer de la Thudinie
      Mirette de la Thudinie            Albionne de Biercee
 Zolla de la Thudinie
            Int. Ch. Soprano de la Thudinie
                                        Joris du Ble d'or
      Ucaba                             Mirette de la Thudinie
      Rakina de la Thudinie             Kiou del Roque du Moulin
                                        Mirette de la Thudinie
```

CH. ODELETTE DU POSTY ARLEQUIN, AKC WA997400, female, whelped Mar 2, 1965
    breeder - F. Grulois

```
                                        Cendrillo de L'Ile Monsin
      Ch. Hion de la Thudinie           Demoiselle de la Thudinie
 Ch. Job de la Thudinie                 Bonzo L'Ideal de Charleroi
      Hulotte de la Thudinie            Flambee de la Thudinie
 Moka de la Thudinie                    Bonzo L'Ideal de Charleroi
      Heros du Posty Arlequin           Eliane de la Thudinie
 Kania de la Thudinie                   Ch. Argus ke la Thudinie
      Demoiselle de la Thudinie         Canaille de la Thudinie
```

CH. ODELETTE DU POSTY ARLEQUIN

```
                                        Cendrillo de L'Ile Monsin
      Ch. Hion de la Thudinie           Demoiselle de la Thudinie
 Ch. Job de la Thudinie                 Bonzo L'Ideal de Charleroi
      Hulotte de la Thudinie            Flambee de la Thudinie
 Liska du Posty Arlequin                Volpi de la Vallee de L'Ecaille
      Ch. Argus de la Thudinie          Ucaba
 Eliane de la Thudinie                  Ygor des Coudreaux
      Canaille de la Thudinie           Zolla de la Thudinie
```

CH. PRUDHON DES PREUX VUILBAARD, AKC WA846769, male, whelped Nov. 5, 1966

                        Ch. Hion de la Thudinie   Cendrillo de L'Ile Monsin
            Ch. Job de la Thudinie   Demoiselle de la Thudinie
                        Hulotte de la Thudinie   Bonzo L'Ideal de Charleroi
    Ch. Marc de la Thudinie   Flambee de la Thudinie
                        Ike de Belgique   Fricko de Belgique
            Remado's Kitty   Erna de Belgique
                        Irisa de L'Ile Monsin   Ch. Ely
                                                         Ch. Balta de L'Ile Monsin

CH. PRUDHON DES PREUX VUILBAARD

                        Ch. Job de la Thudinie   Ch. Hion de la Thudinie
            Lais du Posty Arlequin   Hulotte de la Thudinie
                        Idole du Posty Arlequin   Fricko de Belgique
    Ch. Nota du Posty Arlequin   Eliane de la Thudinie
                        Ch. Job de la Thudinie   Ch. Hion de la Thudinie
            Lolo du Posty Arlequin   Hulotte de la Thudinie
                        Eliane de la Thudinie   Ch. Argus de la Thudinie
                                                         Canaille de la Thudinie

CH. DEEWAL BENJAMIN, AKC WB384749, male, whelped Jul. 31, 1968, breeder -
    Dorothy Walsh

                        Cendrillo de L'Ile Monsin   Urmin du Gratte-Saule
            Ch. Hion de la Thudinie   Tamia de L'Ile Monsin
                        Demoiselle de la Thudinie   Ch. Argus de la Thudinie
    Ch. Job de la Thudinie   Canaille de la Thudinie
                        Bonzo L'Ideal de Charleroi   Ver L'Ideal de Charleroi
            Hulotte de la Thudinie   Xanthane
                        Flambee de la Thudinie   Ch. Argus de la Thudinie
                                                         Canaille de la Thudinie

CH. DEEWAL BENJAMIN

                        Hardy L'Ideal de Charleroi   Bonzo L'Ideal de Charleroi
            Ch. Deewal Lorenzo   Civette L'Ideal de Charleroi
                        Ch. Deewal Argusette   Ch. Argus de la Thudinie
    Ch. Deewal Altesse   Ch. Faussette L'Ideal de Charleroi
                        Hardy L'Ideal de Charleroi   Bonzo L'Ideal de Charleroi
            Bel. Ch. Irca de la Thudinie   Civette L'Ideal de Charleroi
                        Demoiselle de la Thudinie   Ch. Argus de la Thudinie
                                                         Canaille de la Thudinie

CH JASPER DU CLOS DES CERBERES, AKC WB809389, male, whelped Jun. 29, 1970
    breeder - Miss E. Bowles

                        Ch. Marc de la Thudinie   Ch. Job de la Thudinie
            Ch. Picard des Preux Vuilbaards   Remado's Kitty
                        Ch. Nota de la Thudinie   Lais du Posty Arlequin
    Brabo du Clos des Cerberes   Lolo du Posty Arlequin
                        Ike de Belgique   Fricko de Belgique
            Ch. Remado's Katleen   Erna de Belgique
                        Irisa de L'Ile Monsin   Ch. Ely
                                                         Ch. Balta de L'Ile Monsin

CH. JASPER DU CLOS DES CERBERES

                                                         Ch. Coquin de la Thudinie
                        Ch. Chef de Truff   Ch. Draga de la Thudinie
            Ch. Schandor du Clos des Cerberes   Ike de Belgique
                        Ch. Remado's Katleen   Irisa de L'Ile Monsin
    Ch. Altair du Clos des Cerberes   Ch. Rostan du Clos des Cerberes
                        Ch. Telstar du Clos des Cerberes Ch. Remado's Katleen
            Ch. Aurega du Clos des Cerberes   Hardy L'Ideal de Charleroi
                        Deewal Marzie's Lamb   Ch. Deewal Katona

CH. LE BOEF DE CHARDONY, AKC WC 337516, male, whelped Feb. 23, 1971
breeder - Peter Smith

```
                Deewal Max            Bel Ami du Clos Des Cerberes
            Prince                    Yhelot
                Escaut de Belgique    Ch. Argus de la Thudinie
        Grenadier Brian               Coquette de la Thudinie
                Grenadier Alfego de la Vons  Ch. Erlo de la Thudinie
            Grenadier Danseuse        Escaut de Belgique
                Kara du Posty Arlequin  Ch. Hion de la Thudinie
                                      Iota du Posty Arlequin
```

CH. LE BOEF DE CHARDONY

```
                Ch. Gentleman Jim Gent  Ch. Carmel Truffe
            Friar Tuck                Deewal Dione
                Deewal Argusara       Ch. Argus de la Thudinie
        Grenadier Lady Kara           Ch. Fausette de la Thudinie
                Grenadier Alfego de la Vons  Ch. Erlo de la Thudinie
            Ch. Walden's Etranger     Escaut de Belgique
                Kara du Posty Arlequin  Ch. Hion de la Thudinie
                                      Iota du Posty Arlequin
```

CH. DEEWAL VICTOR, AKC WC275903, male, whelped Aug. 10, 1972, breeder -
Justin Chastel

```
                Ch. Quiar de la Thudinie  Ch. Naris du Posty Arlequin
            Ringo de la Thudinie      Naia de la Thudinie
                Nolette de la Thudinie  Ch. Marc de la Thudinie
        Tapin de la Thudinie          Kania de la Thudinie
                Lais du Posty Arlequin  Ch. Job de la Thudinie
            Nina de la Thudinie       Idole du Posty Arlequin
                Lina du Gratte-Saule  Ch. Hion de la Thudinie
                                      Hermine de la Thudinie
```

CH. DEEWAL VICTOR

```
                Ch. Olaf de la Thudinie  Ch. Marc de la Thudinie
            Rico de la Thudinie       Remado's Lisbeth
                Maya de la Thudinie   Lais du Posty Arlequin
        Silette de la Thudinie        Hulotte de la Thudinie
                Ch. Olaf de la Thudinie  Ch. Marc de la Thudinie
            Quelly de la Thudinie     Remado's Lisbeth
                Lina du Gratte-Saule  Ch. Hion de la Thudinie
                                      Hermine de la Thudinie
```